Is There a Culture War?

THE PEW FORUM DIALOGUES
ON RELIGION AND PUBLIC LIFE

E.J. DIONNE JR. AND MICHAEL CROMARTIE
Series Editors

THE PEW
FORUM
ON RELIGION
& PUBLIC LIFE

This book series is a joint project of the Pew Forum on Religion & Public Life and the Brookings Institution. The Forum (www.pewforum.org) delivers timely, impartial information on issues at the intersection of religion and public affairs and serves as a neutral venue for discussing these important issues. The Pew Forum is a nonpartisan organization and does not take positions on policy debates. Based in Washington, D.C., it is directed by Luis Lugo and is a project of the Pew Research Center.

The Pew Forum Dialogues on Religion and Public Life are short volumes that bring together the voices of scholars, journalists, and policy leaders engaged simultaneously in the religious and policy realms. The core idea behind the dialogues is a simple one: There are many authentically expert voices addressing important public questions who speak not only from their knowledge of the policy issues, but also from a set of moral concerns that are often shaped by their religious commitments. The goal is to deepen public understanding of the issues by inviting these voices to join in a dialogue.

Is There a
Culture War?

A Dialogue on Values and
American Public Life

James Davison Hunter

Alan Wolfe

PEW RESEARCH CENTER
BROOKINGS INSTITUTION PRESS
Washington, D.C.

Copyright © 2006

THE BROOKINGS INSTITUTION

PEW RESEARCH CENTER

Library of Congress Cataloging-in-Publication data

Hunter, James Davison, 1955–

Is there a culture war? : a dialogue on values and American public life / James Davison Hunter, Alan Wolfe; comments by Morris P. Fiorina, Gertrude Himmelfarb; E.J. Dionne, Michael Cromartie, editors.

    p.   cm. — (The Pew Forum dialogues on religion and public life)

Includes bibliographical references and index.

ISBN-13: 978-0-8157-9515-5 (pbk. : alk. paper)

ISBN-10: 0-8157-9515-7 (pbk. : alk. paper)

1. United States—Civilization—1970– 2. Culture conflict—United States. 3. Religion and politics—United States. 4. Pluralism (Social sciences)—United States. I. Wolfe, Alan, 1942– II. Title.

E169.12.H773 2006

973.92—dc22   2006028227

2 4 6 8 9 7 5 3 1

The paper used in this publication meets minimum requirements of the American National Standard for Information Sciences—Permanence of Paper for Printed Library Materials: ANSI Z39.48-1992.

Typeset in Adobe Caslon

Composition by R. Lynn Rivenbark
Macon, Georgia

Printed by Victor Graphics
Baltimore, Maryland

CONTENTS

Contents

FOREWORD

IN AN AMERICA that seems increasingly divided between red states and blue states, pro-lifers and pro-choicers, right-wing radio hosts and left-wing bloggers—yet an America where citizens still stand together, hands on hearts, to join in the singing of "The Star-Spangled Banner" at countless sporting events every day—what can we conclude? Is the anthem a symbol of our national tradition and of our shared history that unites us despite our differences? Or are those differences so fundamentally incompatible that we as citizens will be at constant battle against our ideological opposites? Did the collapse of the New Deal coalition and the rise of religious conservatism in the 1970s and 1980s lead to a permanent change in the dynamics of our political system, replacing divisions based on economics and class with those based on cultural and moral disagreements?

This book brings together many of the seminal voices in the study of American culture, partisanship, and values to try to answer these difficult questions. The editors of this volume—*Washington Post* columnist and my Brookings colleague E. J. Dionne Jr. and Michael Cromartie, vice president of the Ethics and Public Policy Center—have structured the discussion as an exchange between experts who bring scholarly research and calm yet thought-provoking arguments to a debate that usually has emotions roiling. They have brought together two formative thinkers in the culture war debate, James Davison Hunter of the University of Virginia and Alan Wolfe of Boston College. No two scholars have had more impact on the topic, and encapsulating their perspectives within one volume is an invaluable contribution to the ongoing discussion. Their dialogue has been strengthened through the commentaries of Gertrude Himmelfarb, author of *One Nation, Two Cultures: A Searching Examination of American Society in the Aftermath of Our Cultural Revolution*, and Morris P. Fiorina, who has recently written *Culture War? The Myth of a Polarized America*.

While differing on some other issues, Hunter and Wolfe both agree that elites are responsible for the existence of the culture war debate. They argue that the elites within our society, and the organizations, denominations, and associations that they lead, have an unequal influence over the products that constitute our culture. Some politicians have been quick to agree. As Spiro Agnew said of his role as vice president under Richard Nixon, "dividing the American people has been my main contribution to the national political scene. I not only plead guilty to this charge, but I am somewhat flattered by it." One does not need to look far to find politicians and activists today who would be similarly boastful of their success in dividing the electorate and "rallying the base."

For her part, Gertrude Himmelfarb, one of our distinguished discussants, challenges the very foundations of the culture war debate by questioning what actually constitutes our culture. She suggests that popular culture is often unaffected by the raging debate in the political sphere and that victories or setbacks in the political culture have not necessarily led to similar changes on the popular culture front, or vice versa. Our second discussant, Morris P. Fiorina, also shakes the foundations of the debate by pointing to evidence suggesting that the orthodox-versus-progressive battle still ranks second to traditional economic issues. He argues that "the divide between poorer and more affluent Americans in partisanship and voting has increased in recent decades, not decreased."

In the midst of these competing pulls, there is the broad mass of moderate Americans trying to live, work, and vote in today's polarized environment. Whether the very nature of our political system naturally tends toward culture war or whether we are coming to the end of a transitory period of political polarization is a question on which this volume's contributors hold differing views. But by presenting these views as part of a respectful dialogue, these essays show that even the biggest differences can be productively addressed in a manner that does not naturally lead to the poisonous atmosphere we have too often seen lately. Rather than expand existing fissures, we hope this volume will help distill the current trends in American culture and its underlying values—how they are formed, by whom they are influenced, and in which ways they are expressed in the opinions of the American public—and, in so doing, perhaps even offer lessons toward lessening our current extreme, suffocating political environment.

This is the fifth volume in the series of Pew Forum Dialogues on Religion and Public Life, which aims to bring intellectuals, policy experts, and civic leaders together to discuss the relationships between faith, values, and politics. The Pew Forum dialogues do not seek to impress a particular viewpoint on readers or to suggest that there is only one answer to the questions posed. In an area of public life where lines are often drawn sharply and harden quickly, the dialogues take the opposite approach. This series encourages public discussion and debate through dialogue. It is intended to open the debate, not narrow it, in the collegial spirit that defines Brookings scholarship. We are grateful for the support of the Pew Charitable Trusts, an organization that has generously supported so many creative projects at our institution.

It is customary to close with a disclaimer: the opinions expressed in this volume are those of the authors alone and do not necessarily reflect the views of the Pew Forum on Religion & Public Life, the Pew Charitable Trusts, or the trustees, officers, or staff of the Brookings Institution. But this volume, like the ones before it, exemplifies Brookings's dedication to addressing the serious and often divisive issues facing our country through reflection, deep knowledge, and openness to the views of others. In the discussion of values, opinions are often colored by emotion and deeply held beliefs. Our hope in publishing this book is that we can open people's minds to a topic very close to their hearts.

STROBE TALBOTT
President, Brookings Institution

September 2006
Washington, D.C.

ACKNOWLEDGMENTS

James Davison Hunter would like to thank Patrick LaRochelle and Emily Raudenbush for their invaluable research assistance. He is also very grateful to his colleagues Joseph Davis, Jennifer Geddes, Charles Mathewes, John Owen, and Murray Milner for their critical reading of these essays.

Alan Wolfe would like to thank E.J. Dionne and Michael Cromartie for engaging him and the other contributors in this debate.

The editors are extremely grateful to Strobe Talbott, president of the Brookings Institution, for his deep and energetic commitment to this project. To Pietro Nivola for his leadership and support as director of the Brookings Governance Studies program; to Tom Mann, Bill Galston, and other Brookings colleagues for their wise contributions; to Katherine Moore and Korin Davis for helping in countless ways to bring this volume to life; to Bethany Hase for administrative assistance; to Robert Faherty, the director of the Brookings Institution Press, who never fails us, embraces our projects, and always offers wise advice; to Janet Walker and Starr Belsky for being patient, careful, and kind editors; to Inge Lockwood for proofreading; to Enid Zafran for indexing; and to Susan Woollen and Sese Paul Design for creating such a striking cover design for this book and for the other volumes in the dialogue series.

We are also grateful to Rebecca Rimel, president of the Pew Charitable Trusts, and Luis Lugo, director of the Pew Forum on Religion and Public Life, for their visionary support for this work. Luis Lugo maintains a steadfast commitment to the most serious research in the area of religion and politics. He is smart, engaged, and cares passionately about the issues at the core of the Pew Forum and this dialogue series. We are also indebted to Sandy Stencel. As the Forum's associate director, Sandy works with warmth, understanding, great intelligence, and a passionate love for words. We are grateful for all the talents she brings to our projects. We are grateful as well to Burke Olsen for his assistance and to all our other colleagues at the Pew Forum. We also offer warm appreciation to our friends and colleagues Kayla M. Drogosz and Jean Bethke Elshtain, coeditors of the earlier volumes in this series.

Above all, the editors owe a tremendous debt to our authors. They bring to the discussion years of insightful reflection and exceptional research. Together, they have created a discourse even more valuable than the sum of their wise contributions.

Is There a Culture War?

INTRODUCTION

⫘

MODERNIST, ORTHODOX, OR FLEXIDOX?
WHY THE CULTURE WAR DEBATE ENDURES

E. J. DIONNE JR. AND MICHAEL CROMARTIE

ON AUGUST 17, 1992, conservative writer and former presidential candidate Pat Buchanan roused the faithful at the Republican National Convention in Houston by declaring war—a very particular kind of war. "There is a religious war going on in our country for the soul of America," Buchanan declared. "It is a cultural war, as critical to the kind of nation we will one day be as was the Cold War itself."[1]

With that speech Buchanan might have rallied the socially conservative faithful to President George H. W. Bush's reelection campaign against Bill Clinton. But many voters in the year of "it's the economy, stupid" were not longing for the cultural struggle to which Buchanan was inviting them to repair. Not only liberal Democrats but also many Republicans disliked the imposition of a martial metaphor on America's cultural and moral disputes. As the *Washington Post* reported, an uneasy Senator Richard G. Lugar told reporters the next morning that Buchanan's "was not an appealing message at all, not a winning message." The Indiana Republican added, "I hope we can focus on the economic issues, rather than cultural wars."[2]

It was probably unknown to Lugar—or, for that matter, to most who heard Buchanan's speech—that the fiery conservative writer was not the person who first put the culture war metaphor into wide American circulation. A year earlier a soft-spoken, tough-minded sociologist from the

1

University of Virginia named James Davison Hunter published a book destined to change the American discussion of cultural politics. *Culture Wars: The Struggle to Define America* argued that there was a battle raging between the orthodox, committed to "an external, definable and transcendent authority," and the progressives, "defined by the spirit of the modern age, a spirit of rationalism and subjectivism."[3]

The traditionalists attracted to orthodoxy, Hunter has always insisted, cannot be dismissed simply as reactionary or backward looking. The "order of life sustained by this vision is, at its best, one that seeks deliberate continuity with the ordering principles inherited from the past." Traditionalists, again at their best, longed for "the reinvigoration and realization of what are considered to be the very noblest ideals and achievements of civilization."[4]

Progressivists, as Hunter called them, had noble ideals of their own, holding a view that "idealizes experimentation and thus adaptation to and innovation with the changing circumstances of our time." Their goal was "the further emancipation of the human spirit and the creation of an inclusive and tolerant world."[5]

Writing before talk radio, cable television, and the Internet became the forces they are today, Hunter described the future (and may have given many clues to Karl Rove and other political maestros in their organization of political campaigns). Hunter wrote that the culture war

> is rooted in an ongoing realignment of American public culture and has been institutionalized chiefly through special purpose organizations, denominations, political parties, and branches of government. The fundamental disagreements that characterize the culture war . . . have become even further aggravated by virtue of the technology of public discourse, the means by which disagreements are voiced in public. In the end, however, the opposing moral visions become, as one would say in the jargon of social science, a reality *sui generis*: a reality much larger than, and indeed autonomous from, the sum total of individuals and organizations that give expression to the conflict. These competing visions, and the rhetoric that sustains them, become the defining forces of public life.[6]

Hunter also made a point that has since become conventional wisdom in the study of religion's relationship to politics. He was one of the first to observe, as Father Andrew Greeley pointed out in his review of *Culture Wars* in the *New York Times Book Review*, "that differences across denominational lines are now less important than differences within denominations." The new religious alignment Hunter described, Greeley noted, is one in which "the orthodox within each tradition are more likely to share values and causes with the orthodox from other traditions than with the progressives within their own traditions."[7]

This means, as recent election results have shown, that conservative Catholics tend to vote with conservative Protestants, while liberal Protestants, liberal Catholics, and liberal Jews are similarly inclined to vote the same way. In a sympathetic account of Hunter's argument, Thomas Byrne Edsall noted that "past splits often pitted upper-class Protestants against working class, ethnic Catholics, placing Elliot Richardson and Tip O'Neill on opposite sides of the fence." But in "today's culture wars," Edsall wrote, "the orthodox Jew may well discover he shares more common ground on critical issues with the evangelical fundamentalist than with the reform Jew or the mainline Episcopalian."[8]

Some years after Hunter's book appeared, Grant Wacker, a professor of religious history at Duke University Divinity School, observed that "one of the most remarkable changes of the twentieth century is the virtual evaporation of hostility between Protestants and Catholics." Wacker was right, and one key to the shift was the new cultural politics described by Hunter. As Wacker noted dryly, the change in Protestant attitudes toward Catholics came in response to social and political issues, and not "because Baptists have come to have a great respect for Tridentine theology."[9]

In one sense the thesis of Hunter's book came to be accepted as the conventional wisdom. Having watched the rise of religious conservatism in the late 1970s and 1980s, many journalists and political activists were prepared to accept that the orthodox-versus-progressive battle was the defining struggle in American politics, and that it had come to replace the economic class alignments of the New Deal era.

But in another sense, the Hunter thesis was contested from the beginning. Yes, there were big cultural battles in America. Yes, members of the

American Civil Liberties Union and members of the Christian Coalition disagreed fundamentally, were in fierce contention, and basically could not stand each other. But wasn't the United States a fundamentally moderate country with a great big middle? Were not most Americans constantly seeking a balance between rights and obligations, between social concern and self-reliance? Were we not best described, in the richly evocative phrase offered by the political philosopher William Galston, as "tolerant traditionalists?"[10] One the authors of this introduction once suggested that America's cultural values are "a rich and not necessarily contradictory mix of liberal instincts and conservative values."[11] Aren't most of us complicated, somewhat conflicted moderates of that sort, more inclined to avoid culture wars than to fight them?

It is a mark of Hunter's importance that he has called forth so many admirers and so many challengers. But the most powerful alternative to the Hunter thesis—although not directly presented as such—was Alan Wolfe's *One Nation, After All*. Published in 1998, Wolfe's book actually was, as its epic subtitle suggested, a quest to find out "what middle class Americans really think about God, country, family, racism, welfare, immigration, homosexuality, work, the right, the left, and each other."[12]

By no means did Wolfe disagree with Hunter on everything. On the contrary, his description of the politics of culture was similar to Hunter's. He saw, as Hunter did, that contemporary American conservatism could

> literally be defined as the defense of middle-class morality, an effort to protect the traditional neighborhoods, family beliefs, work ethic, schools, love of country, and security concerns of the lower middle class, no matter how impoliticly expressed, from the welfare state on the one hand and the liberal defense of modernity on the other. From such a perspective, middle-class morality is good; the only thing that is bad is its continual decline.

By contrast, Wolfe wrote, liberals saw "a world without fixed moral guidelines" as "one that offers individuals greater choice." He continued:

> As conservatives rallied to a defense of the middle-class morality they associated with hardworking sobriety, liberals responded by finding traditional neighborhoods hostile to excluded racial minori-

ties, traditional religiosity hostile to non-believers, and traditional families first oppressive to women and later to homosexuals. Because they identify so strongly with those who are outsiders in the world of tradition, American intellectuals and activists on the left have never had much sympathy for the middle-class morality praised by the right. The left tends to believe that middle-class morality is bad, and the only good thing is that it might become obsolete.

That is a pretty fair description of a culture war. But when Wolfe started interviewing middle-class people, he discovered something interesting. He posed the question directly: "Should we therefore conclude that America is experiencing a culture war?" He replied, "My answer is yes—*but it is one that is being fought primarily by intellectuals, not by most Americans themselves.*" (The emphasis is Wolfe's.) After interviewing middle-class Americans in eight localities across the United States, he concluded that the bulk of the middle class would be inclined to rebuke conservatives and liberals alike. At a Pew Forum conference organized in advance of the release of this book, Wolfe noted "that it is not a division between red state and blue state America; it's a division inside every person."[13] Middle-class Americans can worry about moral decline without being intolerant. They "want the moral scales balanced without being loaded down to one side." They believe, as William Galston wrote in summarizing Wolfe's argument—not surprisingly, Galston found it congenial—in "a morality based on personal experience rather than abstract norms," a morality that is "resolutely modest and unheroic," more "pacific" than "martial."[14] As Wolfe concludes in *One Nation,*

the single most important difference between the practitioners of the morality writ small so prevalent in middle-class America and the morality writ large so characteristic of ideological politics is this: the former want to believe that we can become one nation, after all. And they worry that the ideological proclivities of extremists of left and right will make us two nations—or more—in spite of ourselves. . . . The people who have spoken in this book have no monopoly on virtue. But they do understand that what makes us one nation morally is an insistence on a set of values capacious enough to be inclusive but demanding enough to uphold standards of personal responsibility.

So which is it, a culture war or one nation, after all? In trying to understand what is happening in the United States, should our emphasis be on the sharp disputes that regularly arise in local and national public squares on abortion, gay marriage, and end-of-life issues, on matters of how our children should be educated and the role of religion in public life? Or should we instead pay heed primarily to the vast American middle and its temperamental and spiritual desire for moderation?

The dialogue presented here is designed to shed light on these questions. The editors of the series are deeply grateful that two of the most important thinkers in this debate have agreed to join forces under one book cover to share their insights, their areas of agreement, and their disagreements. Both editors of this volume have had the pleasure of working with Hunter and Wolfe over the years in projects related to religion, community, and public life. For many years we had hoped to bring together two thinkers whom we greatly admired in an extended conversation because each of us thinks that there is considerable truth in the assertions that both Wolfe and Hunter make. We believed that inviting Hunter and Wolfe to sharpen their dialogue would do a great deal to move the nation's conversation on politics, culture, and religion forward. In discussions of morality, values, and virtue, it is often very difficult for the competing sides to hear each other above the din of their own (understandable) passion. Wolfe and Hunter have many virtues, one of which is a capacity to listen closely to what competing parties in the debate have to say and to pay attention. They are both models of the engaged social scientist: they care profoundly about the direction of their country's civic and political life, but they are also able to step back to analyze fairly and insightfully the views of those with whom they disagree. That spirit—of passion and engagement but also of detachment and fairness—is reflected in these pages.

We are also grateful that two other brilliant voices in the culture war debate, historian Gertrude Himmelfarb and political scientist Morris Fiorina, have joined this discussion. They, too, reflect competing points of view.

Himmelfarb, the author of many widely acclaimed books, including *One Nation, Two Cultures,* is not afraid to defend ideas that others might condemn as "prudish, old-fogyish, and—horrors!—judgmental."[15] Interestingly, she challenges not only liberals (and Wolfe) but also her own conservative allies for their eagerness to declare an end to a cultural battle that she believes continues to rage. As she comments here, "Conservatives (or as James Hunter puts it, 'traditionalists') may be winning the war over one sense of the culture, that measured by indices of crime, violence, illegitimacy, and the like. But they are losing the other war, the war over the popular culture—losing it by default, by sheer, willful inattention."

Fiorina comes at the discussion from a very different angle of vision. The lead author of *Culture War? The Myth of a Polarized America*, an important recent contribution to this debate, Fiorina insists that the culture war really is an elite phenomenon and "never had much of a mass base."[16] And he worries that this elite obsession distorts politics and discourages participation. Voters, he says, "are presented with polar alternatives—outlaw abortion or abortion on demand—when they would prefer something in between."[17] Elites, he says, "indulge in cultural battles—abortion, gay rights, gun control, the flag, the pledge, Terri Schiavo, stem cells—as if these were the most important problems facing the country, when polls consistently show that voters consider these minor issues." At the same time, Fiorina argues strongly for more research and more serious thinking about the importance of religion in American politics. "The ratio of casual generalization about religion and politics to grounded research findings," he writes, "is higher than it should be in an academic discipline."

That last thought explains one of the central purposes of the Pew Forum on Religion and Public Life and the inspiration behind its dialogue series, of which this is the fifth volume. In the first volume, *Lifting Up the Poor: A Dialogue on Religion, Poverty, and Welfare Reform*, Mary Jo Bane and Lawrence M. Mead brought together their deep expertise on public policy questions with their profound and reflective faith commitments. That volume was followed by *Is the Market Moral?: A Dialogue on Religion, Economics and Justice* by Rebecca M. Blank and William McGurn, on the obligations to bring moral judgments to our commercial endeavors. *One Electorate under God?: A Dialogue on Religion and American Politics* took on the broad question of faith's relationship to political engagement. Anchored in a discussion between former New York governor Mario

Cuomo and Representative Marc Souder of Indiana, the volume brought together a wide array of voices on a subject that is, if anything, even more vital to the public debate now than it was when the book was first published. And in *Liberty and Power: A Dialogue on Religion and U.S. Foreign Policy in an Unjust World*, six distinguished authors—Father J. Bryan Hehir, Michael Walzer, Louise Richardson, Shibley Telhami, Charles Krauthammer, and James Lindsay—grapple with the new moral imperatives of foreign policy since the terrorist attacks of Sept. 11, 2001.[18] Both of us wish to express profound gratitude to two wonderful colleagues, Jean Bethke Elshtain and Kayla Drogosz, who worked on those earlier books.

The editors of this volume have their own views of the culture war that we have expressed elsewhere. (As would be expected of friends who find themselves on opposite sides in politics, we agree on some things and disagree on others.) But we have worked together for many years in the belief that discussions of religion, politics, and culture can be carried out in the spirit captured well by a writer we both admire, Glenn Tinder. Tinder argued that advocates of freedom, whatever their philosophies or ideologies, should join together to build what he called "the attentive society," a place "in which people listen seriously to those with whom they fundamentally disagree." An attentive society, Tinder insisted, "would provide room for strong convictions, but its defining characteristic would be a widespread willingness to give and receive assistance on the road to truth."[19]

In no area is that injunction more appropriate or necessary than in our discussion of the culture war—assuming, of course, that there is a culture war.

Notes

1. Patrick J. Buchanan, "1992 Republican National Convention Speech," Houston, Texas, August 17, 1992 (www.buchanan.org/pa-92-0817-rnc.html [July 2006]).

2. David S. Broder, "Coherent Message Elusive; At Halftime, GOP Hunts for Theme," *Washington Post*, August 18, 1992, p. A1.

3. James D. Hunter, *Culture Wars: The Struggle to Define America* (New York: Basic Books, 1991), p. 44.

4. See Hunter's essay in this volume, p. 14.

5. Ibid, p. 15.

6. Hunter, *Culture Wars*, pp. 290–91.

7. Andrew M. Greeley, "With God on Their Sides," *New York Times Book Review*, November 24, 1991.

8. Thomas Byrne Edsall, "Culture Wars: The Struggle to Define America. Review," *Washington Monthly* 23, no. 12 (1991): 51.

9. As quoted in E. J. Dionne Jr., "A Shift Looms; The President Sees Consensus, While Religious Leaders Disagree about the Church-State Divide," *Washington Post*, October 3, 1999, p. B1.

10. William A. Galston, "Home of the Tolerant," *Public Interest* 133 (1998): 116.

11. E. J. Dionne Jr., *Why Americans Hate Politics* (New York: Simon and Schuster, 1991).

12. For this and subsequent quotes from Wolfe, see Alan Wolfe, *One Nation, After All: What Middle Class Americans Really Think about God, Country, Family, Racism, Welfare, Immigration, Homosexuality, Work, the Right, the Left, and Each Other* (New York: Viking Penguin, 1998).

13. For a full text of the Hunter and Wolfe dialogue, see Pew Forum on Religion and Public Life, "Event Transcript: Is There a Culture War?" May 23, 2006 (www.pewforum.org/culture-war [July 2006]).

14. Galston, p. 116.

15. Quotes here are from Himmelfarb's comments in this volume. See also Gertrude Himmelfarb, *One Nation, Two Cultures* (New York: Knopf, 1999).

16. Morris Fiorina, Samuel J. Abrams, and Jeremy C. Pope, *Culture War? The Myth of a Polarized America* (New York: Pearson Longman, 2005).

17. This and subsequent quotes are from Fiorina's comments in this volume.

18. See Mary Jo Bane and Lawrence M. Mead, *Lifting Up the Poor: A Dialogue on Religion, Poverty, and Welfare Reform* (Brookings, 2003); Rebecca M. Blank and William McGurn, *Is the Market Moral?: A Dialogue on Religion, Economics, and Justice* (Brookings, 2004); E. J. Dionne Jr., Jean Bethke Elshtain, and Kayla Meltzer Drogosz, eds., *One Electorate under God?: A Dialogue on Religion and American Politics* (Brookings, 2004); and J. Bryan Hehir and others, *Liberty and Power: A Dialogue on Religion and U.S. Foreign Policy in an Unjust World* (Brookings, 2004).

19. Glenn Tinder, "The Spirit of Freedom: To Live Attentively," in *Being Christian Today*, edited by Richard John Neuhaus and George Weigel (Washington: Ethics and Public Policy Center, 1992), pp. 152–53.

THE ENDURING CULTURE WAR

JAMES DAVISON HUNTER

LIBERALISM, AS A philosophical movement and cluster of political ideals, is rooted in the challenges of difference. Liberalism was, in large part, an attempt to provide a humane solution to the difficulties posed by the coexistence of a plurality of dissimilar communities in shared political order. The differences that originally animated liberalism were differences of the most profound sort, those over competing understandings of the good and the sources by which those understandings are known and practiced—most important, religious and metaphysical differences. It is a conundrum indeed when individuals and communities hold competing views of the good that they regard as sacred and, therefore, nonnegotiable. Historically speaking, tension, intolerance, conflict, oppression, violence, and carnage are the natural outcomes of this dilemma. No wonder that difference and diversity have continued to bedevil the best minds in political theory over the last three centuries.

The question of liberalism provides one important context for exploring the debate over the culture war because the subtext of this debate is, in fact, the question of difference in our own time and the conflict that such diversity engenders. To pose the question, "Is there a culture war?" is,

I would like to thank Patrick LaRochelle and Emily Raudenbush for their invaluable research assistance on this essay. I am also very grateful to my colleagues Joseph Davis, Jennifer Geddes, Charles Mathewes, Murray Milner, and John Owen for their critical reading of the piece.

implicitly, to ask a prior question, "Are there politically significant differences operating here?" If so—and in this debate, that is a huge "if"—what is the nature and meaning of the differences involved? And what is the historical significance of these differences?

As it has always been, what is at stake in these questions is liberalism itself as it seeks to offer, in ever new and challenging contexts, a framework for toleration, freedom, and justice. Who is a member of the political community? Whose voices are taken seriously and whose grievances are legitimate? When new claims are made and criticisms expressed, how do the institutions of liberal democracy integrate them and mediate them?

In some ways, the story of liberal democracy in America could be told in terms of the expansion of difference and the way the institutions of democracy have ultimately incorporated those differences into the shared political community. Time and again, the ideals and habits of liberalism have been tested by communities, traditions, and interests seeking a reconfiguration of existing understandings of legitimate difference. Over the last century and a half, Catholics, Jews, women, African Americans, Hispanics, a range of other ethnic minorities, and homosexuals have all challenged the established order, and though circumstances are far from perfect, few would disagree that the range of legitimate difference has been expanded and that conditions for each group have dramatically improved.

In the last half of the twentieth century, it was widely presumed that distinctions of faith and religious community had been largely settled and were thus no longer politically important. The Catholicism of John F. Kennedy in the 1960 election was the exception that proved the rule, and in this sense, it was the last gasp of a dying fear. In the main, the sense prevailed that every religious faith had been domesticated through its relegation to the private sphere. The diversity that mattered now was a diversity of race, ethnicity, class, gender, and sexual orientation. These have occupied an enormous amount of time and attention over the last forty to fifty years and, as I mentioned, to great effect.

But something unexpected is suggested by the idea of a "culture war," especially as it was first articulated. It suggests that the contours of difference have changed yet again in ways that raise a troubling possibility:

though configured in ways that are unfamiliar and possibly unprecedented, perhaps religious and moral differences remain politically consequential in late modern America after all. Perhaps, long after it was
thought settled, the normative differences rooted in sacred cosmologies
(and the communities in which they are embedded) have come to challenge the project of liberal democracy again.

The Culture War Hypothesis . . .

In the late 1980s, I became curious about two phenomena. The first was
a question about whether seemingly disparate social, moral, and political
issues were tied together in some way. What do the arts have to do with
abortion? What does the protest against nuclear power or smoking in
public places have to do with gay rights? Studies had been done on separate issues and separate movements, but there seemed to be points of sym-
metry and even connection that were not being explored or discussed.
Was there something at play in these disparate issues that linked them
together? Many of these conflicts were playing out in local settings around
the country with no connection to each other; yet across the range of
issues, the lines of division were similar, the rhetorical strategies and cultural motifs were comparable, and the patterns of engagement were alike.
Might there be a cultural thread that could make sense of this confusing
jumble?

The second phenomenon concerned who was lining up on different
sides of different issues and why they were doing so. One does not have
to know much about American or Western history to know that when
Protestants, Catholics, and Jews are talking and working together and
even forming alliances in unusual and contradictory ways, that something
counterintuitive and perhaps unprecedented is taking place. Given the
appalling legacy of anti-Catholicism and anti-Semitism in the United
States alone, these developments were remarkable and, on the face of it,
historically significant.

Something was going on, but how best to account for it?

One of the central questions of sociological theory concerns how a
social order is constituted and legitimated. To be sure, categories rooted in
economic and class interest—the categories of "left" and "right"—were

useful as long as they reflected the dominant axis of political tension. But with the collapse of state socialism abroad and the disarray of the labor movement, philosophical Marxism in the academy, and Keynesianism at home, the explanatory power of those categories had weakened, to say the least. Indeed, it is striking just how inadequate social class as a variable (or, for that matter, the categories deriving from political economy) is in accounting for variance in this conflict—in general and in the particulars. This has been particularly true in the United States. The axis of tension that the terms left and right originally described was just not as salient in making sense of political conflict and social change as it once was.

Neither was standard demographic analysis, the staple of sociological practice. Education and residence accounted for some part of the variance, as did gender, though there were highly educated and moderately educated people on all sides of these issues. Similarly, urban dwellers could be found on all sides of these issues, and women were also divided on most of these social issues (and not insignificantly, on abortion). One could find associations in age and occupation, but these too were weak. All ages and all occupations could be found taking most every position. None of these factors individually or together offered a coherent explanation.

Nor could any of these older models explain the passion, commitment, and sacrifice of the actors involved. Something was going on that mainstream social science was either ignoring or for which it could not provide a good explanation. The argument about the culture war was an attempt to address this puzzle.

The heart of the culture war argument was that American public culture was undergoing a realignment that, in turn, was generating significant tension and conflict. These antagonisms were playing out not just on the surface of social life (that is, in its cultural politics) but at the deepest and most profound levels, and not just at the level of ideology but in its public symbols, its myths, its discourse, and through the institutional structures that generate and sustain public culture.

Thus underneath the myriad political controversies over so-called cultural issues, there were yet deeper crises over the very meaning and purpose of the core institutions of American civilization. Behind the politics of abortion was a controversy over a momentous debate over the meaning of motherhood, of individual liberty, and of our obligations to one another. Within the politics of government patronage, including the dispute over the National Endowment for the Arts and its funding of controversial art, one could find a more consequential dispute over what constitutes art in the first place and the social ideals it symbolically communicates. Beyond the politics of educational curriculum, the quarrels over textbooks in public schools constituted a more serious disagreement over the national ideals Americans pass on to the next generation. Behind the contentious argument about the legal rights of gays and lesbians was a more serious debate over the fundamental nature of the family and appropriate sexuality. Within the politics of church and state, the various (and seemingly trivial) altercations over Ten Commandment presentations on public property overlaid a more significant debate about the role of religious institutions and religious authority in an increasingly secular society. And so it goes. Cumulatively, these debates concerning the wide range of social institutions amounted to a struggle over the meaning of America.

This, however, was not the end of the matter. Underneath the push and pull of these institutional conflicts were competing moral ideals as to how public life ought to be ordered and maintained. These were not mere political ideologies, reducible to party platforms or political scorecards, but rather moral visions from which the policy discussions and political disputes derived their passion. Embedded within institutions, these ideals were articulated in innumerable ways with every conceivable nuance and shade of variation. *As they were translated into the signs and symbols of public discourse*, however, they lost their complexity and nuance and thus divided into sharply antagonistic tendencies.

One moral vision—the traditionalist or orthodox—is predicated upon the achievements and traditions of the past as the foundation and guide to the challenges of the present. Though this vision is often tinged with nostalgia and is at times resistant to change, it is not simply reactionary, backward looking, or static. Rather, the order of life sustained by this vision is, at its best, one that seeks deliberate continuity with the ordering principles inherited from the past. The social end is the reinvigoration and realization of what are considered to be the very noblest ideals and achievements of civilization.

Against this is a progressivist moral vision that is ambivalent to the legacy of the past, regarding it partly as a useful point of reference and partly as a source of oppression. Instead, the order of life embraced by this vision is one that idealizes experimentation and thus adaptation to and innovation with the changing circumstances of our time. Although sometimes marked by traces of utopian idealism, it is not merely an uncritical embrace of all things new. The aim of the progressivists' vision is the further emancipation of the human spirit and the creation of an inclusive and tolerant world.

But here, too, there is more to say. Underneath the public policy disputes, the institutional crises, and the conflicting moral visions, there were and are different and competing understandings of what is real and the means by which we can know what is real, and of what is good and true and the means by which we can know these things. Here, too, among citizens and within institutions, one can find nearly infinite variations. As these have become transformed into a grammar of public discourse, however, one can discern two different and competing impulses. Animating one side of the cultural divide is a sense of ultimate reality that is rooted in transcendent authority. Whether apprehended through the foundations of nature or religion or tradition, one can discern and articulate relatively fixed, even eternal, standards through which we can justly organize our personal and collective existence. Animating the other side of the cultural divide is a sense of ultimate reality that rejects the possibility of fixed standards outside of human experience, privileging instead that which we can apprehend through our senses from our personal experience. By these lights, what is real or what is good is not so much constant and enduring but rather much more personal and dependent on the particularities of context.

In sum, at the root of this conflict are competing understandings of the good and how the good is grounded and legitimated. These understandings are reflected in competing moral visions of collective life and the discourse sustaining those visions. In turn, these are manifested in competing institutions (their elites and their interests) that generate this cultural output. All of this plays out dialectically.

Another way to say this is that against the old axis of tension and conflict that was rooted in political economy, a "new" axis of tension and conflict has emerged that is fundamentally cultural in nature. The historical significance of this new axis has been evident in the ways in which it cuts across age-old divisions among Protestants, Catholics, and Jews. The orthodox traditions in these faiths now have much more in common with each other than they do with progressives in their own faith tradition, and vice versa. The polarity of *this* axis seems to better account for the variation in positions on a wide range of popular domestic disputes. In turn, it is the polarities of *these* controversies through which a far-reaching struggle for national identity is carried on.

It is important to bracket the modifier "new" when describing these tensions because they have existed and become institutionalized in the West since at least the mid-1700s. For the most part, however, these tensions remained isolated within fairly remote philosophical discourse, arcane ecclesiastical disputes, or, at most, legal conflict over the constitution of the state. It is only since the 1960s and 1970s that these tensions have played out within popular domestic politics.[1] The historical significance of these tensions, however, could be measured by a realignment taking place within the larger public culture. The politically significant distinctions in American public religion and culture, it seemed, were no longer those between Protestants, Catholics, Jews, and secularists, as they had been for several centuries. Rather, the more salient distinction was between orthodox and progressivist impulses and tendencies within major religio-philosophical traditions. The result has been a historically unprecedented set of alliances among conservative religio-cultural factions and among progressivist religio-cultural factions that have played out in public policy disputes and in opposing nationalist rhetoric.

Given the Enlightenment-based assumptions about intellectual discourse in the last century, it is counterintuitive to suggest that "religion" is at all relevant to a discussion about the ordering of public life. But the institutional manifestations of religion merely point to the normative foundations by which any society, including late twentieth-century America, is constituted and legitimated. As Emile Durkheim, Max Weber, Karl Marx, and Georg Simmel well understood, religion—broadly defined as systems of sacred meaning—was *anything* but irrelevant to the dynamics of conflict and change in the nineteenth century. Broadly conceived, the culture war hypothesis proposes that it remains just as central today.

. . . *and Its Critics*

Not long after the culture war hypothesis was laid out, a small cottage industry of academic sociologists and political scientists emerged to counter the argument. Over the years, the criticism has been substantial and emphatic. The position is unwavering and resolute: no mincing of words and few, if any, qualifications. Steven Brint declared flatly, "There is no culture war in America."[2] Christian Smith and colleagues stated that "the culture war is a myth."[3] Paul DiMaggio and his colleagues concluded that, with the exception of abortion, there was "no support for the proposition that the United States has experienced dramatic polarization in public opinion on social issues."[4] According to Nancy Davis and Robert Robinson, the image of warring factions locked in struggle "is simply false." There is no "monolithic conservative phalanx marching lockstep to the tune of such groups as the Christian Coalition."[5] Ultimately, they declared, the culture war "exists mainly in the minds of media pundits, leaders of political movements, and academics."[6] Such stark demarcations of cultural difference do not—indeed *cannot*—exist, as Randall Balmer noted, because of the "relative absence of ideology in American politics, culture, or religion."[7] Jeremy Rabkin made a similar case for "the culture war that isn't."[8] Alan Wolfe concluded in a like manner, noting that there "is little truth to the charge that middle-class Americans, divided by a culture war, have split into two hostile camps."[9] Wayne Baker echoed this view, saying "that the culture war is largely a fiction."[10] In the latest in this run of criticism, Morris Fiorina declared what had already been said many times before: "The culture war script embraced by journalists and politicos lies somewhere between simple exaggeration and sheer nonsense. There is no culture war in the U.S.—no battle for the soul of America rages, at least none that most Americans are aware of."[11] The polarizing impulses of the culture war are, then, a fabrication. The obverse, in fact, is true. As Wolfe put it, America is "one nation, after all." As such, the time has since long come for social observers to "move beyond the culture war."[12]

In answer to the question about the nature and significance of the wide-ranging social and cultural issues playing out in public life, then, these critics argued, in effect, that nothing of particular consequence was occurring at all. These controversies have no particular meaning and, therefore, do not need further examination, exploration, or discussion because there is no significant normative conflict in America. No alternative explanations are needed because there are no politically consequential religio-cultural differences in America. And all of these categorical judgments were being made in the context of the Clarence Thomas Senate confirmation controversy (a foreshadowing of the current debates over Supreme Court justices); the sex-saturated politics of the impeachment of the forty-second U.S. president; the rise of Fox News and its overt politicization of television journalism; the polarizing dynamics of three presidential elections, including the ongoing realignment of the major parties; and the continuing battles over gay rights that have included thirteen state referendums outlawing gay marriage, not to mention innumerable local controversies around the country that divided churches, schools, neighborhoods, and communities.

How does one explain such stark disagreement over the existence, much less the meaning, of cultural conflict? There are at least three areas that bear further scrutiny. The most obvious concerns the conceptual and methodological differences that may be at play. Are different positions in the debate over the culture war actually referring to and assessing the same thing? The second area is the empirical reality. What are the critics focusing upon and what are they ignoring in order to make their case? The third area concerns the theoretical assumptions brought to bear on the subject of cultural conflict and whether those assumptions are realistic and credible.

Conceptual and Methodological Considerations: The Nature and Meaning of Culture

One explanation for the striking divergence of opinion has to do with *culture* itself—that which is, or perhaps is not, "at war." What is the nature of culture? How do social scientists understand it conceptually and approach it methodologically?

One common way of thinking about culture is in terms of the prevailing values and norms found in a society. These norms and values are composed of the attitudes and opinions, beliefs, and moral preferences of individuals. Culture, then, is the sum total of attitudes, values, and opinions of the individuals making up a society. This view of culture became especially popular among social scientists in the 1950s and 1960s. New developments in public opinion surveys at that time reinforced this approach by providing more refined techniques for sampling average Americans and recording their personal points of view. One school of thought in this vein regarded culture and personality as roughly symmetrical, as mirroring each other. In this view culture was little more than the personality of its individual members writ large, its modal character type or types; understanding culture, in turn, provided a window on the psyche of its individual members. Even after the "culture and personality" studies went out of fashion, survey research and the view of culture it implied remained a dominant approach to culture in the social sciences.

As much as survey research had advanced the understanding of social life, by the late 1970s and early 1980s, American sociology was beginning to recognize the weaknesses of this approach to culture. The methodological individualism implied in survey methods came to be seen by many as narrowly conceived, limited in scope, reductionistic in its claims, and, in the end, facile in its explanations. In general, the view that culture was simply the sum total of subjective attitudes and opinions of ordinary people was seen as inadequate by itself to account for the complexity of culture. Surveys proved important to social analysis, but alone they were insufficient to explain the intricacies of social life.

At the same time, American cultural sociology discovered afresh the contributions and relevance of neoclassical, structural, and poststructural approaches to the study of culture that had been established and further developed in Continental and British social theory.[13] This led to a greater focus on the patterns of culture, its institutional dimensions, its production within organizations, the artifacts it produced, the resources mobilized behind it, the elites who wielded disproportionate influence in articulating the guiding narratives, and so on. It also gave impetus to understanding public symbols and rituals, public discourse, the unspoken structures of authority, and how all of these things relate to the formation of collective identity and to the public philosophies and shared narratives that legitimate its claims.

It is in the context of this evolving history in social science and the changing conceptual and methodological strategies for understanding culture that we begin to see how two different positions on the culture war debate have emerged. To wit, all of the empirical tests of the culture wars hypothesis—*all of them*—have been based exclusively upon individual-level data from either public opinion surveys or face-to-face interviews. The result has been predictable: on the whole, American public opinion simply did not reflect the divisions described by the argument of deep normative conflict. Paul DiMaggio and his colleagues, for example, reviewed survey data from the General Social Survey (GSS) and the National Election Studies (NES) from the early 1970s to the mid-1990s and found that, with the exception of abortion, there was "no support for the proposition that the United States has experienced dramatic polarization in public opinion on social issues."[14] Davis and Robinson also drew from the GSS and concluded that "most Americans occupy a middle ground between the extremes."[15] A dissertation by Yonghe Yang in 1996 covered much the same ground in the GSS (from 1977 to 1996) and found "no hint of ideological dichotomy."[16] Wolfe interviewed dozens of people from eight different communities and found much the same.[17] Smith and his coworkers conducted in-depth interviews of 128 individuals and found that most people were oblivious to the very concept of a culture war, and among those who had heard of it, most were disdainful of the idea.[18] Baker's work was based upon the World Values Survey, and Fiorina's study was based primarily on a review of analyses of GSS, NES, and Gallup public opinion data.[19] In sum, all of the criticisms of the culture war hypothesis were based on an implicit view of culture and an older form of cultural analysis that were, to say the least, limited from the outset.

Collective psychology is fine as far it goes; it can teach much about the patterns and trends of opinion and belief. But the argument about a culture war in America was based upon a different understanding of culture, one that was strongly influenced by the structural turn in cultural analysis. This turn viewed culture not as the norms and values residing in people's heads and hearts but rather as systems of symbols and other cultural artifacts, institutions that produce and promulgate those symbols, discourses that articulate and legitimate particular interests, and competing fields where culture is contested. For my own part, the heart of the culture war hypothesis was the contention that there had been a realignment in American public culture that had been and still is institutionalized chiefly through special interest organizations, denominations, political parties, foundations, competing media outlets, professional associations, and the elites whose ideals, interests, and actions give all of these organizations direction and leadership. These dynamics played out in different ways in different cultural fields. In all, the dynamics of collective identity formation—the necessity for an "other" to clarify the moral boundaries of the group and reinforce the moral authority of its elites—added force to the polarizing impulses at work. Even further, the polarizing tendencies of competing fields of cultural production were aggravated by the technologies of public discourse. Through these structural developments and processes, competing moral visions and the conflict itself have become, in Durkheim's phrase, a reality *sui generis*, a reality much larger than—indeed, autonomous from—the sum total of individuals and organizations that give expression to the conflict. It was and is only at this level that the term *culture war*—with its implications of stridency, polarization, mobilization of resources, and so on—has its greatest conceptual force.[20] It explains, among other things, how it is that our public discourse becomes disembodied from (and hence larger than and independent of) the individual voices that give it expression. In this way it explains how our public discourse becomes more polarized than Americans as a people are.

It is true that some critical commentary never engaged the scholarly works that put forward the idea of cultural conflict but rather focused on the popular usage of the term.[21] While one would think that the scholars' more sophisticated understanding of a popular concept would invite a more rigorous conceptualization and analysis, this was not the case. As such, references to popular treatments tended to slide seamlessly into citations of more scholarly sources, with the net effect being to render suspect any use of the term *culture war*. In the end many of the critics created a straw man that then proved relatively easy to knock down.

The problem is, none of the critics addressed the *culture* in culture wars. None of them examined the question of the culture war from the theoretical, conceptual, or methodological approaches of the new sociology of culture. None examined the structures of culture that produce and distribute symbols, ideas, arguments, and ideologies; their social location and their interests; their implicit formulations of moral authority; the antagonistic discourses; and so on. Rather, every criticism was based upon the most narrow and constricted conceptualization of culture, thus looking for conflict where the conflict has always been weakest (for example, the average opinions found in public opinion). From this came the authoritative conclusion that politically consequential normative conflict was simply nonexistent. Not to put too fine a point on it, the culture war argument has always been about culture, in all its complexity of meaning within the social sciences, and the conflict that continues to unfold in, around, and through it—and not about conflict over the attitudes and opinions of average Americans. It is in this way that the critics have overstated their case. Their data simply cannot support the conclusion that significant *cultural* conflict is nonexistent and, therefore, imaginary.

A False Debate?

On the face of it, then, the disagreement between those who propose and those who reject the culture war hypothesis would seem to be conceptual and methodological, not substantive in nature. Given such differences in approach, it is difficult to imagine that there would not be differences in conclusion.

That said, it must also be noted that many of the empirical assessments of public attitudes have been quite serious, perceptive, and helpful. With the exception discussed later in this essay, it is difficult not to agree with much of what has been written about the popular sentiment of average Americans. Within the actual limits that their data allow, there is little to dispute.

For my own part, I have spent considerable effort elaborating these very insights. In my earliest work on evangelicals, I found among these most conservative of Americans strong tendencies toward accommodating liberal modernity; not only in their attitudes toward the family, work, and the self but in their understanding of Scripture and core beliefs. In *Culture Wars* I acknowledged again and again the prevalence of complexity and nuance outside the framework of the polarizing tendencies, and an entire chapter was devoted to the way in which the voices of the majority in the middle are eclipsed.[22] For the book *Before the Shooting Begins*, I drew from a national survey of opinion involving face-to-face interviews with over 2,000 Americans to explore the complexity of public attitudes toward abortion—the consummate culture wars issue.[23] The middle, it turns out, is quite diverse in its views. On the abortion issue, about 65 percent of the population hold positions in between the extremes, and though not radical in any of their views, neither were their views a muddle, as many have thought. There is a very interesting structure to public opinion among Americans who occupy the middle ground on this issue that represents neither polarization nor consensus.

In 1996 the Institute for Advanced Studies in Culture sponsored another survey of political culture in America and found a similar dynamic in the middle that reflected neither contented harmony nor seething discord.[24] My colleague Carl Bowman and I approached the question of the middle from a slightly different vantage point here.[25] Our objective was to go beyond what people think is right or wrong regarding different issues to determine the framework of people's commitments to public culture and, in this way, to explore how the public is divided in its normative commitments. By "framework of people's commitments," we meant the terms by which the *moral* is conceived by individuals—for themselves personally and the larger society. We constructed indexes that measured key moral priorities: the relative commitment to self versus others, to universal truth versus particular (and relative) truths, and to traditional moral codes as guidelines for one's life.[26] We then performed a cluster analysis to identify subgroups of the population that differ significantly in their core commitments.

We found a remarkable range of moral diversity between the extremes of traditionalism and permissivism. Roughly 15 percent of the population can be characterized as *conventionalists*—a moderate-to-conservative group whose cultural orientation seems to be more a matter of form and longstanding practice than conviction. About 14 percent can be loosely characterized as *pragmatists* who tend to be traditional in their moral beliefs and understanding of truth but who are the least self-sacrificial and most hedonistic of all. Finally, about one-fifth of the population was *communitarian*. In general, communitarians are religious liberals who, while fairly skeptical about traditional morality and epistemology, are distinctive in their desire to subordinate personal gain on behalf of collective needs or interests. Within this complex pattern of normative diversity, we found factions operating with very different moral languages and conceiving of their public commitments in different ways. Moreover, they tend to view opposing sides in complex ways. They find the elites of the progressive left appealing, in many respects, for they embody the American dream of achievement, security, and mobility; they symbolize the success of the system. At the same time, the average American is put off by their aloofness, arrogance, and perceived self-interestedness. By contrast, the Christian right has appeal within the larger public for its patriotism and its defense of a traditional middle-class work, moral, and familial ethic. Yet the public is simultaneously repelled by what it perceives as the Christian right's rigidity, intolerance, and extremism.

To be sure, the relationship of the larger public to American political culture is exceedingly complex. My own contributions to understanding average Americans "in the middle" are in sympathy with precisely what the critics of the culture wars hypothesis have found. But this does not mean that there are no politically significant cleavages in the culture—or in popular opinion, as it turns out.

Empirical Considerations: The Social Composition of Dissensus

To find significant difference in the general population, one has to know where to look for it and then explore its meaning in relation to the larger social order. What, then, can be said for the true believers on each side within the general population?

First, the data set of choice for many of the criticisms of the culture wars hypothesis was the General Social Survey, and as most social scientists acknowledge, the GSS is at best a crude instrument for evaluating public opinion. This is especially true regarding dissensus, since few if any of its questions thoughtfully target the subsamples that make up contesting factions or have been written with the substantive issues of conflict in mind. That said, it is clear even from these data that there are substantial minorities within the American public whose moral and political orientations are strikingly at odds. Their attitudes and opinions also divide much like one would expect from the discourse of the culture wars.

Though one can haggle over precise figures, virtually everyone agrees that somewhere between 10 and 15 percent of the population occupy these opposing moral and ideological universes.

There are different ways of slicing the pie. For example, in terms of political self-identification, the *1996 Survey of American Political Culture* found 9 percent who identified their politics as very liberal to far left and 12 percent who described their politics as very conservative to far right. It is a start but, of course, also a fairly crude measure. Regarding specific issues that constitute the politics of the culture war, one also finds approximately 8 to 12 percent who take strong and uncompromising positions on one side or another. They are not always the same people, but the percentages work out about the same from issue to issue.

Still another way to slice the pie is to combine various moral, religious, and political factors to identify the strongly committed partisans of the Christian right and of the progressive left. Here again, by conservative estimates, these individuals constitute about 5 to 7 percent of the population on each side. Partisans on each side strongly affirm their commitment to American political ideals and are highly involved in civic and political affairs, having significantly more ties to various associations than those who occupy the middle ground.[27] However, individuals in each faction have a very different understanding of the world and their experience in it. They are, in some of the most significant ways, "worlds apart." In our analysis of the *1996 Survey of American Political Culture*, Bowman and I found that there were some differences in social class (with progressives in the upper middle class and conservatives in the middle of the middle class) but less than one might think. Partisans on each side also operate with distinct and fundamentally different understandings of the moral life and moral authority: one group operates from a biblical foundation that tends toward absolutism that reinforces traditional values, while the other tends toward moral improvisation and, in rare instances, relativism that predisposes its members to ambivalence toward traditional moral codes.[28] While both factions strongly affirm the ideals of the American democratic tradition, they understand this tradition differently; at key points they are at odds in their understanding of American history and purpose, and work with different interpretations of the American creed.[29]

Not least is the degree to which each faction is self-conscious of the other and, as such, self-consciously antagonistic toward the other.[30] Majorities in each faction view the other as hypocritical, characterless, self-serving, insensitive to the concerns of most Americans, out of the mainstream, out-of-touch with reality, and undemocratic.[31]

To broaden the analysis, one can look at those who form the larger base, whose view of the world is sympathetic with the most strongly committed partisans though not nearly as resolutely or as coherently. One fruitful way to approach this is not in political terms but rather in terms of how people make sense of moral reality. In the cluster analysis mentioned earlier, Bowman and I found roughly one-fourth of the population who could be called traditionalists (or neotraditionalists) and about one-fourth who could be called permissivists.[32] The traditionalists and neotraditionalists are, in terms of their commitment to traditional morality, self-sacrifice, and a belief in absolutes, the most conservative people in America today. The traditionalists are overwhelmingly and conservatively theistic in their religious stances and operate with a providentialist view of American history; the neotraditionalists are much the same though they differ by virtue of their better education, urban residence, and representation among racial and ethnic minorities. Inhabiting a fundamentally different moral universe are the permissivists, who make up about 27 percent of the American population. These individuals are perhaps the most secular of all Americans, the most lenient toward traditional morality, the most relativistic toward truth, and among the least self-sacrificial in weighing personal interests against the common good. Urban permissivists tend to be younger and more diverse racially and ethnically compared to their small-town counterparts.

It is clear that within themselves, traditionalists and permissivists do not have political positions that align perfectly with their moral dispositions. Yet the alignment is fairly close, and for this reason these groups represent a natural and broader constituency receptive to political and social mobilization.[33]

The point is this: no matter how one approaches the question, social dissensus is very much present in public opinion. Forming the grassroots support for competing visions are factions that constitute the white-hot core of difference and dissensus. Disproportionately motivated and active in these issues, they are the most likely to write letters, send checks to the special interest groups and parties that represent them, and volunteer on behalf of their cause. Although these highly partisan citizens may only make up 5 percent of the American population on one side of the cultural divide or the other, in actual numbers they account for 10 to 12 million people on each side. Extending out to less committed constituencies, the numbers who align themselves on one side of the cultural divide or the other can range up to 60 million each.

But this still leaves open the question, are these factions and the larger constituencies of which they are a part politically significant? In his review of *Culture Wars* for *Contemporary Sociology*, Steven Brint posed the question this way: "Can one have a proper war when two-thirds of the army are noncombatants?"[34] The answer brings us back to one of the central contentions of the original argument about the culture war: it has everything to do with the institutions and elites that provide leadership to these factions.

The Work of Elites and the Institutions They Lead

Some of the critics of the culture wars hypothesis do acknowledge that there are activists who are engaged in these issues, but they have tended to view them as noisy extremists who have no particular influence. Wolfe isolates the conflict to "intellectuals."[35] Fiorina prefers to call the typical activist an "exhibitionist, crack-pot, blowhard."[36] Smith and colleagues declare the conflict at this level "distant and trivial."[37] Yet because historical or empirical evidence has not been offered, it turns out that these statements are merely opinion. They beg the question, what is the role of elites? What role do the institutions they lead have in a culture? And what of the activists and the movements they constitute?

To take the structural and institutional approach in cultural analysis is, in part, to think of culture as objects produced. Culture takes the form of ideas, information, news—indeed, knowledge of all kinds—and these in turn are expressed in pronouncements, speeches, edicts, tracts, essays, books, film, works of art, laws, and the like. At the heart of the production and distribution of cultural output is language. It is, of course, at the root of culture for it provides a medium through which people experience reality. Through both its structure and its meaning, language provides the categories through which people understand themselves, others, and the larger world around them. The power of language resides in its ability to objectify, to make identifiable and "objectively" real the various and ever changing aspects of our experience. When objects are named, when relationships are described, when standards of evaluation are articulated, and when situations are defined, they can acquire a sense of facticity. For this reason formal education, the media of mass communications (including television, radio, newspapers, magazines, and the like), art and music, and religious pronouncements (such as sermons, edicts, policy statements, moral instruction, liturgies and rituals, and the like) all become important conduits for communication and socialization—mechanisms through which a particular vision of reality is defined and maintained. It stands to reason that influence over language, the cultural output through which public language is mediated, and the institutions that produce and manage it all are extraordinarily powerful.[38]

The development and articulation of the more elaborate systems of meaning and the vocabularies that make them coherent are more or less exclusively the realm of elites. They are the ones who provide the concepts, supply the grammar, and explicate the logic of public discussion. They are the ones who define and redefine the meaning of public symbols and provide the legitimating or delegitimating narratives of public figures or events. In all of these ways and for all of these reasons, it is they and the strategically placed institutions they serve that come to frame the terms of public discussion.[39]

In sum, there are elites who are enormously influential for the sway they have over the content and direction of cultural production within specific institutions. These are supported by 5 to 8 percent of the population who are the grassroots activists, the "cultural warriors" who generate and organize resources on behalf of their respective associations and factions. There are yet larger parts of the population whose fundamental orientation leans one way or another but who also tend to be more moderate and less motivated. Yet they can and are mobilized for action in public affairs (even if only by voting) under certain circumstances.

A Case Study, Repeated Myriad Times

Consider briefly a case concerning school reform in Gaston County, North Carolina, in the early 1990s.[40] The school district there was ranked among the bottom 17 school districts in the state (out of 120) in terms of students' academic performance, high dropout rates, and so on. To rectify this matter, the Board of Education put together the Odyssey Project that incorporated five elements of reform, including a change in pedagogy called "outcomes-based education." The school district won a $2 million grant as the beginning of a $20 million grant in a national competition to implement this reform. Through the work of a local Baptist pastor who drew on the support and materials of Citizens for Excellence in Education (CEE)—a religiously based, special interest organization concerned about secular reforms in the public schools—an opposition was mobilized. The CEE was dead set against outcomes-based education, saying it manipulated and indoctrinated children with secular humanism, New Age thinking, and hostility to Christianity. As its director put it, outcomes-based education marked "the end of academic education in America."[41] It was not long before parents and other citizens "packed school board meetings where they monopolized the use of the microphone, harassed school board members, wrote letters to local newspapers, distributed fliers urging parents to act swiftly in order to save their children from the dire effects of this 'radical' school program, circulated warnings [through email] and gathered signatures on petitions."[42]

Soon enough, another national special interest organization, People for the American Way, became involved in direct ways. People for the American Way claimed that the CEE and other organizations of the religious right posed a dire threat to freedom and tolerance in the United States. Each organization was able to use this local dispute to promote its own larger interests far beyond Gaston County. Neither organization conceded rhetorical space or was willing to consider any compromise. A substantive debate about the merits of the reform proposal never occurred, and in the end, all reform efforts were scuttled, the remaining grant funds were forfeited, the school superintendent was forced to resign, and a community was divided. And still, in the end, it was the children of Gaston County who paid the highest price.

Concluding Observations

The culture war does not manifest itself at all times in all places in the same way. It is episodic and, very often, local in its expressions. Examples abound: the dispute over the fate of Terri Schiavo in Pinellas Park, Florida; the conflict over teaching "intelligent design" in Kansas City; the controversy over a teacher in the Bronx who was suspended for bringing bibles to P.S. 5; a clash over a Civil War statue in Richmond, Virginia; the tempest over a priest in St. Paul who refused to serve communion to gays at Mass; the fury of parents in Mustang, Oklahoma, after the superintendent excised a nativity scene at the end of the annual Christmas play; the dispute over speech codes at the University of Pennsylvania; the row over release time for religious instruction in the public schools in Staunton, Virginia; and on it goes.

Yet because what is under dispute and what is at stake is culture at its deepest levels, carried by organizations relating to larger movements, these local, often disparate conflicts are played out repeatedly in predictable ways. The nation was not divided by the Odyssey Program, but the community of Gaston County, North Carolina, was for a time and profoundly, with serious consequences. So have been and are communities and regions all over the nation whenever an event fraught with moral meaning and cultural significance occurs that compels communities to take positions and make decisions.

Are local and national elites and the organizations they represent politically significant? They certainly were in this instance, and as it has become clear over the years, they are in virtually every other instance of cultural conflict as well. It is in their interest to frame issues in stark terms, to take uncompromising positions, and to delegitimate their opponents. Clearly, entire populations are not divided at anywhere near the level of intensity of the activists and the rhetoric, but because issues are often framed in such stark terms, public choices are forced. In such circumstances even communities and populations that would prefer other options, and much greater reason and harmony in the process, find themselves divided.

There is nothing really new here. It would, in fact, seem to be the pattern with social conflict generally, not least when it becomes violent.

"Total war" is a recent, and relatively rare, phenomenon. Throughout most of human history, war has been a minority affair, involving fractions of the warring peoples' populations and, if only by default, the residents of the regions where the battles were actually joined. The idea that wars (even civil wars) should mobilize entire peoples in support of the war efforts is a distinctively modern orientation.[43] And while the two great examples of this kind of war play strongly upon our imaginations, in the last analysis, even they must be reckoned as exceptional. To the extent that such conflicts do demand more "democratic" participation, our national war efforts are frequently geared toward mobilizing the ambivalent masses. Historically, and even in the present, many of our wars still take place at a remove from the citizens of the warring nations. In the early twentieth century, for example, a mere 5,000 dedicated volunteers fought against the army of the United Kingdom for the independence of the Republic of Ireland.[44] The same dynamic of relatively small cores with larger, potentially polarized and mobilized peripheries can be found in the Russian Revolution in 1917 and the Maoist Revolution in the 1940s. In Rwanda it was the extremist elements of the ruling government and armed forces and the extremist militia who organized the massacre of somewhere between 5 and 10 percent of the population in 1994.[45] In the case of the conflict between Arabs and Jews in Israel and Palestine, it is only a minority at the ideological extremes who are involved in perpetuating the conflict. Indeed, polls show that more than eight out of ten Israelis and eight of ten Palestinians support reconciliation, as a general concept.[46] Needless to say, the opinion of this majority is not reflected in the continued presence of conflict in that area. In this light, it seems hasty to dismiss all talk of a culture war just because the combatants are small as a percentage of the whole. Indeed, would the critics have argued that there was no politically consequential conflict over civil rights or the war in Vietnam because the majority of Americans took middling positions?

To be sure, elites, activists, the institutions they lead and grassroots support they mobilize, and the larger publics that form their natural constituencies are enormously consequential. Yet their importance is not just measured by the power to frame issues. It is also inversely measured by the lack of influence of the majority of Americans, who are in the middle, to contradict this framing and offer an alternative. If the culture war is a myth and the real story is about the consensus that exists in "the middle," then why is it that the middle cannot put forward, much less elect, a moderate who represents that consensus, with all of its complexity and ambivalence on so many issues? If the center is so vital, then why is it that the extremes are overrepresented in the structures of power—not least, political power? In the case of the dispute over educational reform in Gaston County, where was that contented middle—that consensus that critics suggest is so broad and dynamic? In this dispute and in others like it, the middle was there, but as the outcome showed, it was also, sadly, inconsequential.

This, it would seem, helps to explain some of the dynamics at work in the 2004 national election and, indeed, the three or four elections immediately preceding it. Data collected by the Pew Research Center indicate that among white Americans, religio-cultural factors have become among the most important in determining voting preferences in national elections.[47] As the 2004 election demonstrated, Americans who are religiously orthodox and who attend worship services regularly increasingly vote Republican and take conservative stands on the range of cultural policy issues. Conversely, those who are more secular and less connected to religious institutions increasingly vote Democratic and take liberal positions on these same policy issues. Further analysis affirmed a central argument of the original culture wars hypothesis, though now for average citizens:

> The important political fault lines in the American religious landscape do not run along denominational lines, but cut across them. That is, they are defined by religious outlook rather than denominational labels. . . . The survey also found that traditionalists in all three major faith groups overwhelmingly identify with the Republican Party—and that traditionalist Evangelicals do so by a 70 percent to 20 percent margin. The margins among Mainline Protestant and Catholic traditionalists are less lopsided but nonetheless solidly Republican. On the other side of the divide, modernists in all these religious traditions as well as secularists strongly favor the Democrats. Modernist Mainline Protestants, for example, now favor the Democrats by a more than two-to-one margin.[48]

Needless to say, the majority of Americans were not self-conscious partisans actively committed to one side or the other but rather constituted a soft middle that tended one way or inclined toward the other. But the options they ended up with were framed by elites in the parties and special interest organizations, their respective institutions, and the rank-and-file supporters who formed the grassroots support. So, too, were the narratives that contextualized and the arguments that legitimated those choices. Thus, when push came to shove, Americans—even in the middle—made a choice.

Theoretical Reflections on Cultural Conflict

Given their conceptual and methodological starting point, it is not at all surprising that the critics of the culture wars hypothesis focus on collective psychology and the general agreements one can find there. Yet there are theoretical grounds for questioning the narrative of consensus just on the face of it. Put differently, there are good theoretical reasons for assuming just the opposite of consensus—to begin with, the presumption of cultural tension and conflict.

For one, social scientists know that culture is made up of various systems of actors and institutions competing in fields of social life for position, resources, and symbolic capital. This means that culture is, by its very constitution in social life, contested. In a society as pluralistic as ours, the tendencies toward cultural conflict are inevitably intensified because the diversity of actors and institutions in competition has increased. Consciously or not, various actors within our public culture employ strategies and tactics to preserve or expand their ability to shape their field of influence. As always, the stakes are not, at least first, material but rather symbolic: the power of culture is the power to name things, to define reality, to create and shape worlds of meaning. At its most extensive reach, it is the power to project one's vision of the world as the dominant, if not the only legitimate, vision of the world, such that it becomes unquestioned.[49]

And yet the conflictual nature of culture is apparent in an even more basic way than competition over the institutional means of worldmaking. It is a commonplace of structural semiotics that our experience of the world is made meaningful through comparisons and oppositions.[50] A concept, an idea, a proposition, an object, an action, a group, a movement—these by themselves are not inherently meaningful but rather take on significance in relation to their opposite, something other, or in some cases, simply their absence. The meaning of the world, then, takes shape for us within these multiple and wide-ranging oppositions, in relation to the differences we perceive. Light becomes meaningful in relation to dark or haziness; liberty takes on significance in relation to oppression, coercion, or control; abundance makes sense in relation to scarcity, and so on. Our understanding of the world is framed and illuminated by these comparisons. So it is in social life with the formation of collective identity. The self-understanding of a society or a social group is, by the very nature of things, formed dialectically in distinction to other societies or social groups. Collective identity becomes crystallized most sharply, then, in relation to others who are different. The various means of social control (for example, through punishment, litigation, ostracism, opprobrium, name-calling, and the like) highlight these differences and are, in fact, ways in which social groups assert their own collective identity, establish and reestablish their moral authority, reinforce the group's solidarity, and maintain boundaries between insiders and outsiders. This dynamic is a fundamental feature of social life at all levels of complexity or simplicity. Without such boundary work, a social group, a community, a society faces what may be an even greater danger—its own internal moral disintegration.

And thus culture is, by its very nature, contested—always and everywhere, even when it appears most homogeneous. As Philip Rieff has put it, "Where there is culture, there is struggle"; it is "the form of fighting before the fighting begins."[51] This is so even if it is not always reflected in public opinion. And when there is real war, culture is the centermost part of the war itself. It is so because culture provides the terms by which collectivities seek their own survival and the annihilation of the other. Oppositions are totalized and militarized.

Liberalism and Difference

Is there a politically significant normative conflict in contemporary America? Indeed there is. And the only way to conclude that there is no such normative conflict is to reject all but the most limited and superficial conceptualization of culture, disregard massive amounts of evidence (even from survey research), and take little to no account of directions suggested by social theory. Does it amount to something justifying the term "culture war?" This phrase is a metaphor, and the appropriateness of any metaphor is measured by how well it fits the subject it describes. To those engaged in this conflict—the activists who are involved in the divisions and the citizens who get caught up in its logic—this is just the right metaphor. Repeatedly one will hear people say that "war" is exactly what it feels like.

Beyond the significant conceptual issues, the methodological differences, the existence of abundant multidimensional evidence to the contrary, and, not least, the fundamental challenge of social theory, there is something curious about the cumulative argument against politically significant normative conflict. There was, of course, a time when the social sciences were far more attentive to questions of conflict—indeed, when conflict was at the heart of social theory and analysis. Such tendencies are nowhere to be found among the critics of the culture wars. What accounts for the absence of curiosity or even openness to the possibility that this conflict exists and might mean something? The unwillingness to consider well-established conceptual, methodological, and theoretical traditions as ways of approaching normative conflict creates an impression of a profession settled in its ways, comfortable with its predispositions and prejudices, and, perhaps, a bit too defensive. To say that the larger story is really one of consensus is to say, in effect, that all is well; there is nothing to be concerned with in these matters. In its net political effect, this kind of social science looks very much like the establishment and consensus-oriented structural functionalism of the mid-twentieth century. Strange as this seems, this similarity is a minor curiosity compared to its larger significance.

Intended or not, in its net effect, this narrative of consensus also entails a denial of difference. The subtext of this narrative is that if there is no politically or historically significant normative conflict, then there are no differences that need to be accounted for or made sense of or addressed. One need not take seriously the claims or grievances of the other. In this case, the denial of difference is a denial of the particularities in social ontologies that define these normative communities. The ideals, practices, and sources of moral authority that constitute collective identity and solidarity are simply ignored. In social life these are by no means the only

differences among groups, communities, and societies, but they are, perhaps, the deepest differences—differences that often enough engender
hatred and hostility. For the social sciences, this is not merely a lapse but
a missed opportunity. Indeed, on the international scene, we in America
and the West are paying a price for our longstanding blindness to these
deep normative differences.

There is an issue closer to home as well. Liberalism is, among other
things, an attempt to find a way to live together. As a political culture, liberalism not only allows but also protects diversity in its fullest possible
scope. However, a denial of deep difference makes us inattentive to important developments in the social order that, whether people like it or
not, are challenging anew the ideals and institutions of liberalism. This,
too, may be at our peril.

Notes

1. Robert Wuthnow's explanation for this is rooted in the expansion of higher
education. Robert Wuthnow, *The Restructuring of American Religion* (Princeton
University Press, 1988).

2. Steven Brint, "What If They Gave a War . . .?" *Contemporary Sociology* 21,
no. 4 (1992): 438–40.

3. Christian Smith and others, "The Myth of Culture Wars," *Culture: Newsletter
of the Sociology of Culture, American Sociological Association* 11, no. 1 (1996): 1, 7–10.

4. Paul DiMaggio, John Evans, and Bethany Bryson, "Have Americans' Social
Attitudes Become More Polarized?" *American Journal of Sociology* 102, no. 3 (1996):
690–755.

5. Nancy Davis and Robert V. Robinson "Are the Rumors of War Exaggerated?
Religious Orthodoxy and Moral Progressivism in America," *American Journal of
Sociology* 102, no. 3 (1996): 756–87.

6. Nancy Davis and Robert V. Robinson. "Religious Orthodoxy in American
Society: The Myth of a Monolithic Camp," *Journal for the Scientific Study of Religion*
35, no. 3 (1996): 229–45.

7. Randall Balmer, "Culture Wars: Views from the Ivory Tower," *Evangelical
Studies Bulletin* 10, no. 1 (1993): 1–2.

8. Jeremy Rabkin, "The Culture War That Isn't," *Policy Review*, no. 96 (1999):
3–19.

9. Alan Wolfe, *One Nation, After All: What Middle Class Americans Really Think
about God, Country, Family, Racism, Welfare, Immigration, Homosexuality, Work, the
Right, the Left, and Each Other* (New York: Viking Penguin, 1998), pp. 320–21.

10. Wayne Baker, *America's Crisis of Values: Reality and Perception* (Princeton University Press, 2005), p. 109.

11. Morris Fiorina, "What Culture War?" *Wall Street Journal*, July 22, 2004, p. A14. See also Morris Fiorina, Samuel J. Abrams, and Jeremy C. Pope, *Culture War? The Myth of a Polarized America* (New York: Pearson Longman, 2005).

12. Wolfe, *One Nation*, p. 286.

13. Here I speak of the influence of Claude Lévi-Strauss, Roland Barthes, Louis Althusser, Mary Douglas, Michel Foucault, Jürgen Habermas, and Niklas Luhmann, among others. For a summary of these shifts in the study of culture, see Robert Wuthnow and others, *Cultural Analysis: The Work of Peter Berger, Mary Douglas, Michel Foucault, and Jürgen Habermas* (London: Routledge and Kegan Paul, 1984). See also Robert Wuthnow, *Meaning and Moral Order: Explorations in Cultural Analysis* (University of California Press, 1987).

14. DiMaggio, Evans, and Bryson, "Americans' Social Attitudes," p. 738.

15. Davis and Robinson, "Rumors of War," p. 780.

16. Yonghe Yang, "The Structure and Dynamics of Ideological Pluralism in American Religion," University of Massachusetts, 1996. For a revised excerpt, see Yonghe Yang and Nicholas J. Demerath III, "What American Culture War? A View from the Trenches as Opposed to the Command Posts and the Press Corps," in *Civil Wars in American Politics*, edited by Rhys Williams (New York: Aldine de Gruyter, 1997).

17. Wolfe, *One Nation*.

18. Smith and others, "Myth of Culture Wars."

19. See Baker, *America's Crisis of Values*; Fiorina, "What Culture War?"

20. James Davison Hunter, *Culture Wars: The Struggle to Define America* (New York: Basic Books, 1991), pp. 290–91; James Davison Hunter, *Before the Shooting Begins: Searching for Democracy in America's Culture War* (New York: Free Press, 1994), pp. vii–viii.

21. For example, DiMaggio, Evans, and Bryson targeted the rhetoric of then-Senator Warren Rudman, Wolfe pointed to the arguments of Irving Kristol, and Smith and colleagues admitted that they were most concerned with countering "popular conceptions" of the culture war. See DiMaggio, Evans, and Bryson, "Americans' Social Attitudes"; Wolfe, *One Nation*; and Smith and others, "Myth of Culture Wars."

22. Hunter, *Culture Wars*, pp. 159–61.

23. See Hunter, *Before the Shooting Begins*.

24. Unless otherwise indicated, assertions and quotes in the rest of this and the following section are from James Davison Hunter and Carl F. Bowman, *The State of Disunion: The 1996 Survey of American Political Culture, Summary Report* (Charlottesville, Va.: Institute for Advanced Studies in Culture, 1996). The survey was fielded by the Gallup Organization. The sample consisted of 2,047 respondents representative of the noninstitutionalized population of the continental United

States, age eighteen years and older. It was gathered via stratified, multistage probability sampling of households and weighted to ensure representativeness on key demographic characteristics (race, gender, region, age, and education). The interviews were conducted in person and lasted about one and a half hours on average.

25. Ibid., p. 81.

26. The first index, license versus restraint, measured assent to these cultural adages: "Live for today," "Good fences make good neighbors," "Look out for number one," "Money is the key to life's satisfactions," and "Eat, drink, and be merry." The second, defined as relativism versus absolutism, measured acquiescence to such statements as "Everything is beautiful—it's all a matter of how you look at it," "The greatest moral virtue is to be honest about your feelings and desires," and "All views of what is good are equally valid." Relativism scores were then discounted for those who agreed that "Those who violate God's rules will be punished," "It is my responsibility to help others lead more moral lives," and "We would all be better off if we could live by the same basic moral guidelines." The third index, traditional versus progressive morality, measured the degree of each respondent's moral opposition to divorce, premarital sex, sexual relations between two adults of the same sex, interracial marriage, alcohol, smoking cigarettes, smoking marijuana, watching pornographic films, and swearing or using offensive language.

27. The most conservative individuals belong to an average of 5.29 associations, and the most progressive belong to an average of 4.09 associations. The average for those in the middle was 3.53 associations.

28. Hunter and Bowman, *State of Disunion*, pp. 55, 80, 83–95.

29. As we noted, both extremes share an "exceptionalist" view of American history and purpose. Yet they part company in dramatic ways in how they interpret this: the Christian right operates with a strong, providentialist view of history and purpose that progressive social elites just as strongly reject.

30. Hunter and Bowman, *State of Disunion*, pp. 60–62, and James D. Hunter and Daniel Johnson, "Establishment Sociology and the Culture Wars Hypothesis," unpublished working paper.

31. Ibid., pp. 60–63. John Evans updated the DiMaggio study using 2000 data and found that political partisans in the general population were even more divided than ever. Cited in Jonathan Rauch, "Bipolar Disorder," *Atlantic Monthly*, January-February 2005, p. 104.

32. Traditionalists and neotraditionalists constituted 11 and 16 percent of the population, respectively.

33. We compared the groups according to political self-identification (Hunter and Bowman, *State of Disunion*, p. 89) and on a range of specific issues relating to gay rights (Ibid., p. 93). See also Alan Abramowitz and Kyle Saunders, "Why Can't We All Just Get Along? The Reality of a Polarized America," *Forum* 3, no. 2 (2005): article 1 (www.bepress.com/ forum/vol3/iss2/art1 [September 2005]). Their evidence indicates that "there are deep divisions in America between Demo-

crats and Republicans . . . and between religious voters and secular voters. These divisions are not confined to a small minority of elected officials and activists—they involve a large segment of the public, and they are likely to increase in the future as a result of long-term trends affecting American society."

34. Hunter, *Culture Wars*; Brint "What If They Gave a War," p. 440.

35. Wolfe, *One Nation*.

36. Fiorina, Abrams, and Pope, *Culture War?* p. 105.

37. Smith and others, "Myth of Culture Wars," p. 10.

38. See Stephen Lukes, *Power: A Radical View*, 2d ed. (London: Palgrave Macmillan, 2005).

39. See David A. Snow and Robert Benford. "Ideology, Frame Resonance, and Participant Mobilization," *International Social Movement Research* 1 (1988): 197–217, and David A. Snow and Robert D. Benford, "Master Frames and Cycles of Protest," in *Frontiers in Social Movement Theory*, edited by Aldon D. Morris and Carol M. Mueller (Yale University Press, 1992), pp. 133–55. This is the first reason why the vast majority of Americans who are somewhere in the middle of these ·debates are not heard. They have no access to the tools of public culture in the way elites do.

40. This account is fully described in Kimon Sargeant and Edwin L. West Jr., "Teachers and Preachers: The Battle over Public School Reform in Gaston County, North Carolina," in *The American Culture Wars*, edited by James Nolan (University of Virginia Press, 1996), pp. 35–59.

41. Ibid., p. 42.

42. Ibid., p. 41.

43. Maurice Pearton, *Diplomacy, War and Technology since 1830* (University Press of Kansas, 1984).

44. See Peter Hart, "The Social Structure of the Irish Republican Army 1916–1923," *Historical Journal* 42, no. 1 (1999): 207–31. At the height of the fighting—between 1916 and 1923—there were up to 100,000 individuals in the Irish Republican Army, but for the majority of the conflict, there were 5,000 volunteers who were considered "reliable" and "active" (p. 209), and these were "disproportionately skilled, trained, and urban."

45. Extremists in the military and government bitterly opposed the Arusha Accord, a power-sharing treaty for warring factions in Rwanda, and were the likely culprits in the assassination of Rwandan president Juvenal Habyarimana on April 6, 1994. "Within an hour of the plane crash, the Presidential Guard, elements of the Rwandan armed forces (FAR) and extremist militia (*Interahamwe* and *Impuzamugambi*) set up roadblocks and barricades and began the organized slaughter, starting in the capital Kigali, of nearly one million Rwandans in 100 days' time. Their first targets were those most likely to resist the plan of genocide: the opposition Prime Minister, the president of the constitutional court, priests, leaders of the Liberal Party and Social Democratic Party, the Information Minister, and tellingly,

the negotiator of the Arusha Accord." William Ferroggiaro, ed., "The U.S. and the Genocide in Rwanda 1994: Evidence of Inaction," *National Security Archive,* August 20, 2001 (www.gwu.edu/~nsarchiv/NSAEBB/NSAEBB53/).

46. "General support for reconciliation among Israelis has also increased and stands now at 84 percent compared to 80 percent in June 2004. Eighty-one percent of the Palestinians support reconciliation today compared to 67 percent last June. More important, however, is the consistent across the board increase in support for a list of specific reconciliation steps, varying in the level of commitment they pose to both publics." Palestinian Center for Policy and Survey Research, "Joint Israeli-Palestinian Public Opinion Poll, March 2005: Summary of Results," March 16, 2005 (www.pcpsr.org/survey/polls/2005/p15ejoint.html).

47. Pew Research Center, *Trends 2005* (Washington: 2005). See also John C. Green and others, "The American Religious Landscape and the 2004 Presidential Vote: Increased Polarization," Survey report (Washington: Pew Forum on Religion and Public Life, February 3, 2005).

48. Pew Research Center, *Trends 2005*, p. 28. This statement mirrored one made thirteen years earlier in Hunter, *Culture Wars*.

49. Lukes, *Power*.

50. I do not at all subscribe to orthodox structuralist assumptions about duality but fully recognize that objects may have multiple meanings and interpretations depending upon circumstances. See the critique of Claude Lévi-Strauss in Mary Douglas, "The Meaning of Myth, with Special Reference to 'La Geste d'Asdiwal,'" in *The Structural Study of Myth and Totemism*, edited by Edmund Leach (London: Tavistock), pp. 49–70.

51. Phillip Rieff, *Sacred Order/Social Order*, vol. 1: *My Life among the Deathworks* (University of Virginia Press, 2006).

THE CULTURE WAR THAT
NEVER CAME

ALAN WOLFE

EVERYTHING WAS ALL SET. An important assistant to a Republican senator had written the memo demonstrating the benefits his party would receive by taking immediate action. His party's leaders in Congress started drafting legislation and writing their speeches while the Republican president, a man well known for his determination to stay on course, changed his travel plans to fly to Washington at short notice from his Texas ranch. Democrats, meanwhile, struck dumb by the unfolding events, had nothing to say, fearing, once again, that anything they did say would confirm their reputation as liberal elitists insufficiently respectful of the culture of life. Terri Schiavo, a woman who had been kept alive on a feeding tube for fifteen years after her husband and parents disagreed on what her intentions had been, was all set to be one more campaign in the American culture war.

And then, nothing happened—or at least nothing along the lines that nearly all pundits in the United States anticipated. Public opinion polls quickly showed that most Americans, by a 63 to 28 percent margin, supported the removal of Terri Schiavo's feeding tube; that even Republicans were inclined to think along these lines; and that by a 25 percent margin, Americans opposed the decision by Congress and the president to pass and sign a law requiring that the details of one family's tragic situation be once again reviewed by the courts.[1] Although demonstrators continued their vigil outside the hospice where Schiavo lay in her bed, their numbers were small—smaller, sometimes, than the number of journalists covering them. No noticeable rise in anger at judges could be detected throughout the land, despite emotional (and, in the opinion of many, irresponsible) attacks on the judiciary from elected politicians. President Bush tried to change the subject. Majority leader Tom DeLay, by engaging the issue, only called attention to his ethical problems. If either party gained from the fracas, it was the Democrats. Ultimately Terri Schiavo's life ended, and public attention turned to the death of one pope and the elevation of another.

In the 1960s, protestors against Vietnam held placards saying, "What if they gave a war and no one came?" The Terri Schiavo case raises the same question about America's culture war. Americans have heard endless talk about the degree to which they are divided into red states and blue states. They disagree, we are frequently told, about matters involving life and death, issues on which compromise and negotiation are by their very nature impossible. For some Americans, it is widely believed, God offers the only credible authority for answering difficult moral and ethical questions, while for others human beings must use powers of reason and logic bequeathed to them from the Enlightenment. Could it be that in the wake of talk like this, there really is no such thing as a culture war, at least not out there in those places in America where people are just trying to make all those difficult decisions that involve leading a good and meaningful life?

I believe that the Schiavo case is the rule, not the exception. As I argued in my 1998 book *One Nation, After All*, the culture war has always existed more in the minds of journalists and political activists than in the lives of ordinary Americans.[2] This does not mean that there is no such thing as a culture war; it simply means that the one being fought by partisans and ideologically inclined pundits does not extend very deep into American opinion. (In what follows, therefore, any use of the term "culture war" refers to this inside-the-beltway struggle and not to what is taking place in middle America.) The "culture war," in this sense, has always involved less than meets the eye. And now that Americans face serious political issues—terrorist attacks, uncertain allies, nuclear proliferation, and potential economic instability at home and abroad—they are turning away from issues that strike them as manufactured and extremist in favor of evaluating candidates on the basis of more practical criteria such as their character or, odd as it sometimes may seem, their actual positions on issues such as Social Security. Far weaker than typical political commentary portrays it, the culture war is on its last legs, and those who continue to insist on fighting it are likely to find themselves on the sideline in America's political future.

What Terri Teaches Us

Republicans who believed that the Terri Schiavo case would be a winner may have made a political miscalculation, but their error did not originate with the poor woman on the feeding tube and her distraught family. The script for the Schiavo case had been written months earlier when Americans voted in the presidential election of 2004.

At previous periods in American history, the 2004 election would have not been considered particularly unusual. When Americans find themselves at war, they frequently are inclined to reelect a sitting president, especially when he is not held responsible for either the war's origin or its mismanagement. President Bush had made the decision to take the war against terror to Iraq, but for most Americans, the war itself started with September 11, and the president, it was widely believed, was a strong leader demonstrating his resolve to defeat the enemy. And while the war in Iraq had not gone especially well, casualties were far lower than they had been during the Vietnam War, and there seemed to be some progress toward establishing democratic conditions in that country. Under such circumstances, the only surprise registered in the election was its closeness, at least in the electoral college. Despite all the advantages of incumbency, Mr. Bush won because of a relatively small margin in the state of Ohio.

As accurate as such a reading of the 2004 election may be, it was not an especially dramatic one. But just as every World Series has to be the greatest one ever played, the media seemed determined to find a way to call this election one of the most important ever held. Two words enabled them to do so: moral values. "President Bush's victory, the approval of every antigay marriage amendment on statewide ballots, and an emphasis on 'moral values' among voters showed the power of churchgoing Americans in this election and threw the nation's religious divide into stark relief," wrote the Associated Press as soon as the election's outcome was known.[3] The AP's conclusion had been based on an exit poll showing that "moral values" ranked higher than Iraq, terrorism, the economy, and taxes in the minds of voters. As with soccer moms and NASCAR dads, a one-size-fits-all explanation of American political behavior had suddenly appeared on the scene.

When John Kenneth Galbraith coined the term "conventional wisdom," he was referring to ideas that had been so long in circulation that everyone had come to accept them as true. In today's political universe, dominated by instant response focus groups, Internet blogging, and the insatiable demands of cable television, a conventional wisdom can be established in a matter of hours. And so it came to pass. Democrats, conventional wisdom held, had lost because of their support for gay marriage, while Republicans had won because they mobilized their base among conservative Protestants who rank the word of God higher than such mundane issues as jobs or health care. Even as late as May 2005, some writers were still claiming that 20 percent of Americans had made moral values central to their concerns and that such voters understood, as a member of President Bush's Council on Bioethics put it, that "there are limits given us by God and nature to our selfish or individualistic efforts to remake the world to suit our convenience as individuals."[4]

For Galbraith the conventional wisdom was nearly always wrong, about which he may not always have been right, but there is no doubt it was wrong in this case. Just about everything the media proclaimed in the immediate aftermath of the 2004 election was committed to the proposition that in America the culture was not only alive and well but determined the election's outcome. And a substantial part of what they said is now known to be incorrect.

The exit poll upon which the importance of moral values was based, it turns out, was extremely flawed; "moral values" could have meant anything, including concerns that encompassed the other categories with which it was being compared. To correct for that error, political scientists D. Sunshine Hillygus and Todd G. Shields subjected a comprehensive postelection survey to techniques that allowed them to distinguish more carefully the factors that led individual voters to vote the way they did. They found that voters proved to be very loyal to their parties, which meant, for example, that pro-life Democrats and pro-choice Republicans were more likely to vote along partisan lines than according to their views on abortion. When partisan voters did defect from their parties, moreover, their reasons had more to do with the war in Iraq or the state of the economy than with the so-called moral issues. Among independents, as the authors put it, "gay marriage and abortion had no impact on individual vote choice once other factors were controlled." Values played a minor role at best in the election, and the role they played mostly involved reinforcing the determination of those who already supported President Bush to support him more strongly. The conclusion of Hillygus and Shields is striking: "The moral values issues of gay marriage and abortion matter most where the campaign mattered least."[5]

If this conclusion is correct, the results of 2004, far from demonstrating the persistence of the culture war, show the remarkable degree to which the culture war has receded in American life. For one thing, an issue that in the past had been considered an essential part of the culture war—in fact, it was the original "wedge issue" meant to divide Americans from each other—made no significant appearance in 2004: race. By finding a compromise on affirmative action—one that may not have possessed much legal coherence but conformed to the widespread public consensus that special efforts should be made to include minorities in college admissions without relying on rigid quotas—the U.S. Supreme Court simply took the matter off the table. (Along similar lines, President Clinton's support of welfare reform helped dampen partisan controversies over crime and inner-city poverty.) In 1969 it was said that the key to the long-term future of the Republican Party was to develop a "Southern strategy" that would appeal to whites in the South who once voted Democratic.[6] The strategy worked, but race, while important in the transition to the new Republican South, was not, in the end, the divisive issue it once seemed to be. If anything, as important a Republican leader as Mississippi senator Trent Lott had to give up his position as majority leader because of racially insensitive remarks he had made in the past, to be replaced by Tennessee's Bill Frist, who has made his appeal to the conservative base of his party hinge on religious rather than racial concerns.

In the absence of race, the two remaining culture war issues, as Hillygus and Shields rightly observe, were abortion and gay marriage. And if they are correct that neither of those issues was particularly salient to vot-ers, then the only conclusion to reach after the 2004 election is that the culture war had declined in importance since the 1990s, when, if I can refer to my own research, at least one of those issues, gay rights, seemed far more divisive and irresolvable.

Based on 200 long (but not statistically representative) interviews with middle-class Americans in the suburbs of four American cities, I had con-cluded that most Americans remained moderate in their views, even on the so-called moral issues.[7] If there was a culture war, I argued, it took place inside Americans and not between them: Americans believed in both traditional religious values and personal freedom, and it was not always easy for them to decide which was more important. The media and the political class, I suggested, were fighting the culture war for their own reasons; to the degree that Americans expressed a view about that fight, it was not to take sides but to distance themselves from it. They especially did not like matters of private choice becoming issues of public debate. E. J. Dionne Jr. has written about why Americans hate politics.[8] If they do, and if they love God, it made no sense that they would want to see the things that matter to them corrupted by processes they view as divisive and dirty.

One of the earliest decisions I made in developing my interviews was that I would not ask Americans about abortion. This surprised some of those who believe that differences over abortion all but launched the cul-ture war after *Roe* v. *Wade*. But a body of social science evidence had per-suaded me that Americans were not all that divided over abortion and that it therefore made sense not to reexamine a finding so widely ac-cepted. Since the book was published, that consensus has remained intact. By large majorities Americans want women to retain the right to have an abortion, even if they are also willing to allow more restrictions on that choice that *Roe* v. *Wade* initially permitted. In their book refuting the idea of an American culture war, Fiorina, Abrams, and Pope show that these views have changed little over time, do not vary significantly by religious background and gender (or even political party), and that, despite the per-sistent efforts of religious conservatives to promote their position on the issue, there has been more movement toward supporting the basic prem-ise of *Roe* v. *Wade* over time than against it.[9] Their findings help explain why President Bush, who evokes language supporting the culture of life and promises to appoint judges who will apply rather than interpret the Constitution, has never actually taken a position calling for *Roe* v. *Wade* to be overturned. For every conservative Christian vote he might gain by doing so, he would lose many more centrists on this issue.

The discovery that abortion did not play a significant role in the 2004 election, then, comes as no surprise. But the same is not true of the finding that gay marriage failed to rank high on the minds of voters. Unlike abortion, gay rights questions were part of my earlier survey, including a question on gay marriage. On this issue, I concluded, a culture war very definitely did exist. Americans, I found, were deeply divided over gay rights. They tended to support the rights of gays in the private sphere; Americans tend to be libertarians and do not like the idea of government policing what happens in bedrooms. But on public matters—and marriage is a very public matter indeed—they had strong reservations. Out of the mouths of my interviewees came some pretty strong language condemning homosexual lifestyles, words that stood in sharp contrast to the generally nonjudgmental language Americans prefer to use. I did not foresee the prospect of much consensus emerging on this issue in the near future.

Polls continue to show that Americans oppose gay marriage. Moreover, majorities in all eleven states where gay marriage was on the ballot in 2004 voted against it. Even though gay marriage might not have mattered to the results of the presidential election in 2004, as many assumed at the time, it was still important.[10] Surely, then, it is wrong to lump the issue of gay marriage and abortion together; the former still divides Americans much more than the latter. Today, just as in the 1990s, gay marriage would seem to be the great exception to the argument that the importance of the culture war has been exaggerated.

This conclusion, I believe, is at least partially accurate; there remains a fundamental gap between those Americans who believe that marriage should be reserved for a union between men and women and those who believe it should not. Understood in a narrow and technical sense, moreover, the decision by the Massachusetts Supreme Judicial Court to legalize gay marriage may well have helped decide the presidential election of 2004; the margin of victory for Mr. Bush in Ohio was close enough that the presence of an initiative against gay marriage on the ballot may well have pulled just enough votes to the Republican side to swing the election in Mr. Bush's favor. If the culture war exists anywhere, it exists here.

Yet having said all that, it remains remarkable that the position on gay marriage taken by Vice President Cheney in 2004 was to the left of the position originally taken by Howard Dean when he was governor of Vermont: while Dean signed a 2000 bill authorizing civil unions in his state, he did so after some hesitation, whereas Vice President Cheney went out of his way to announce his support for civil unions, even in the face of strong opposition within his party. Moreover, only after a long delay did President Bush support a constitutional amendment to ban gay marriage, and he never supported it with enthusiasm, signaling to all and sundry his discomfort with the conservative position on this issue. (Mr. Bush's decision to reaffirm his support for a constitutional amendment banning gay marriage just before the midterm elections of 2006 was even more cynically presented to the American public.) For all the opposition to gay marriage, there remain many Americans, including many conservatives, who believe that gay people are better off in strong, marriage-like relationships, all of which suggests that a compromise in which gay couples were allowed to form legally binding relationships that nonetheless stopped short of full marriage rights would likely have consensual support.[11] And even though large numbers of Americans may oppose gay marriage on the grounds that marriage is sacred, they also treat the Constitution as sacred and are reluctant to alter it. Gay marriage, in short, is a divisive issue, but it is not as divisive as it was just ten or twenty years ago because public opinion has generally shifted in a more tolerant and nuanced direction.

The 2004 election and the Terri Schiavo case, along with the reluctance of the American public to join in a Christian-right led campaign against "activist" judges, suggest that the American culture war simply does not call all that many troops to battle. True, there are issues, including moral and religious issues, over which Americans are divided, as in a democracy they ought to be. It is also true that American politics has entered a highly partisan period in which negotiation and compromise, the traditional stuff of politics, have become harder to accomplish. But none of this is welcomed by large proportions of the American public, many of whom continue to consider themselves independents, are dismayed by ideological zeal, give low grades to both the president and Congress, and are looking for more moderate and centrist politicians to articulate their sentiments.[12] Culture war issues are unlikely to go away as long as politicians need to mobilize their base and ideologically driven interest groups need to raise funds. But it is likely that Americans in the near future will also be addressing the question of whether they should be having a culture war at all, especially if they tire of the political instability and occasional gridlock that seem to come with it.

In the 1950s and 1960s, political scientists argued that one of the main functions of political leadership was to moderate the more extremist views of ordinary Americans in order to make consensus possible. In the 1990s, by contrast, or so I argued in *One Nation, After All*, ordinary Americans had become more moderate than their leaders.[13] This remains as true in the age of Tom DeLay and Nancy Pelosi as when I wrote it, if not more so. From stem cell research to alleged plots against Christmas, culture war issues have more to do with the policies of advocacy groups than they do with the politics of ordinary Americans.

Where Faiths and Politics Clash

To deny that the culture war resonates with ordinary Americans is not to deny that there exists something *called* a culture war. As long as political elites find value in staking out extreme positions on issues involving fundamental moral values, they will do so, and their efforts will be duly reported by the media and become the fodder for electoral debate and even legislative action. The question to be answered, then, is not whether a culture war exists but why one *continues* to exist, even in the face of substantial public resistance to it.

The culture war represents a situation in which religion and politics meet; issues that once were handled by talking to clergy or through prayer and devotion come to be decided by politicians considering issues of public policy. To understand why culture war issues persist, it is important to appreciate how changes in both politics and religion have brought together two realms of human existence that Americans have generally tried to keep apart.

Recent, and often quite dramatic, developments in American politics have done more than their share to contribute to the persistence of the culture war. Perhaps the most important of them is the fact that the ideological cleavage that once existed *within* each of the major parties now exists primarily *between* them. The Democratic Party coalition hammered in place by Franklin Delano Roosevelt contained liberals from the Northeast and conservatives from the South, while the Republicans had long been divided between East Coast moderates and midwestern and western conservatives. All that has changed in recent years. Once solidly Democratic, the South is now overwhelmingly Republican. And there is the example of Vermont senator Jim Jeffords, a moderate Republican who left the party to become an independent who voted with the Democrats. As late as the elections of 2000 and 2004, Ralph Nader tried to insist that the two dominant parties were not all that different from each other. But they are—no doubt one reason why Nader did so poorly.

Increasing partisan and ideological conflict has given the American political system an almost British-like coherence: a majority can pass legislation important to it, and the minority has little choice but to act as a loyal opposition. This may have momentarily cheered advocates for a more responsible party system in the United States, but lost along the way was the ability of parties to fashion legislation capable of winning bipartisan support in the center of the political spectrum. When the parties were more ideologically blended, patronage and profit tended to be the most important motivations in politics. When each becomes more ideological, activists guided by single-issue causes supply much of the energy that enables the parties to function. The culture war continues because our current ways of doing politics allows considerable scope for culture warriors.

This tendency of the parties to become more ideological has been reinforced by a number of other recent developments in American political life. Sophisticated computer programs make it possible for congressional districts to be drawn in ways that create safe seats for both parties. As if that were not political protection enough, the Republicans opted to draw new districts in Texas even before the customary ten years between redistricting had expired, a development bound to encourage Democrats to retaliate in states in which they hold majorities. When combined with the tendency of Americans to vote for incumbents in the first place, these changes have resulted in fewer contested seats in the House of Representatives; in the 2004 election, 339 of the 435 seats in the House (77.9 percent) were won by candidates obtaining more than 60 percent of the vote. With fewer contested elections, House members, not especially worried about casting unpopular votes that will lead to challenges against them, are freer to vote their ideology, which is increasingly what they do.

The same kinds of impacts can be detected at the presidential level. While presidential campaigns tend to be extremely competitive—look at the close results in 2000 and, at least in the electoral college, in 2004—the important contests are the primary elections that determine who gets nominated for president. Turnout in primary elections tends to be low, which gives disproportionate weight to those candidates who can mobilize ideologically driven followers. A premium is placed on money and organization, which these days are more likely to be supplied by interest groups than by old-fashioned party machines. Advertising takes the place of organized get-out-the-vote drives, and such advertising, inevitably featuring bumper sticker size messages focusing on the negative attributes of one's opponents, plays a more prominent role in campaign strategizing. In 2004 Karl Rove, President Bush's chief political advisor, demonstrated that it was possible to win an election not by appealing to the center but by activating those in the base. That lesson is unlikely to be ignored by future generations of political consultants.

These political changes are reinforced by developments in other kinds of institutions. The media, for example, as recently as the 1950s and 1960s, had viewed themselves as neutral and objective, commenting on politics rather than taking an active, partisan role. No longer is this a widespread view of the media's function. Revisiting the highly partisan political environment of nineteenth-century American politics, the editorial page of the *Wall Street Journal*, the Fox television network, and the myriad "talk radio" outlets that have sprung up all over the country consider themselves openly conservative and proud of their determination to elect Republican candidates. Liberals and Democrats have not been especially successful at matching their efforts, although there are some tentative signs that liberal talk radio may catch on. But even if liberals had just as many listeners, watchers, or readers as conservatives, the change would still be apparent: each would still appeal to its own following, and in the face of such ideological zeal, any kind of objectivity would be inadvertent rather than the result of a commitment to a common or collective good.

Like the media, religious organizations have come to be active participants in the American culture war. Liberal religious groups involved themselves deeply in left-wing causes throughout the 1960s and 1970s, from the civil rights movement to peace movements that opposed the war in Vietnam or America's reliance on nuclear weapons. Today much of that energy has dissipated, but the close connection between religion and left-wing politics persists in many mainline congregations and in the divinity schools at most prestigious American universities. Black churches are still an important element in Democratic Party campaigns, and Reform Jews and social-justice-oriented Catholics remain active participants in liberal politics. Once upon a time in American politics, to be a religious person serving in Congress was to be someone such as Robert Drinan, S. J. (who eventually resigned his seat when the Vatican, which has no principled position against Catholic participation in politics, had a very specific objection to his participation in politics).

As if to prove that politics need not be confined to the religious left, the religious right, from the 1980s to the present, responded in kind. Baptists, the largest Protestant denomination in the United States, have long-standing commitments to religious liberty and the separation of church and state, but this has not prevented the current leadership of the Southern Baptist Convention from openly siding with conservative political voices overwhelmingly sympathetic to the Republican Party. As if to reinforce the message it sent when it asked Father Drinan to resign from Congress, the Catholic Church seems to feel that Democratic involvement in politics is wrong while the same level of Republican involvement is not; a number of American bishops denounced pro-choice Democratic politicians in 2004 but ignored the existence of Republicans with the same pro-choice views. Conservative religious leaders seem to feel that the once-sharp line between religion and politics needs to be redrawn, even if doing so shifts religious focus from otherworldly concerns to the practical details of legislation and judicial appointments. These leaders insist that however important individual salvation may be, attention must be paid to getting the politics of the United States on the right track. The increasing political popularity of the Republican Party is too great an opportunity for them to resist, and they have made it clear that resisting it is something they are not prepared to do. Their efforts all but ensure that religion and politics will continue to blend, especially as leftists and liberals, both wary and envious of conservative success from the pulpit, urge similar objectives from their end of the political spectrum.[14]

Any war, including a culture war, requires at least two sides. At the time of its origin, America's culture war had them. Liberals, in fact, may have begun the culture war: their decision to prevent the appointment of Robert Bork to the Supreme Court was accompanied by heated rhetoric about Bork's views that inflamed a desire for revenge on the part of those who admired his positions on issues such as abortion.[15] The conservative charge that liberals could not win popular majorities for their positions on cultural issues, and that they therefore had to rely on courts or administrative agencies to get what they wanted, rings true. It is quite understandable that Americans who objected to liberal gains attained in such an undemocratic manner would seek to reverse them by appealing to the popular majorities on their side. Liberals did themselves no favor by arguing, as New York University law professor Ronald Dworkin did, that in any conflict between rights and democracy, the former should trump the latter.[16]

But it has also become clear that since the 1980s liberals and Democrats have not moved nearly as far to the left as Republicans and conservatives have moved to the right. Positioning herself for a possible presidential bid, Hillary Clinton moved to the center on nearly all major issues from abortion to Iraq, thereby provoking opposition from left-wing bloggers. Conversely, to position himself for the same goal, Bill Frist moved sharply to the right, speaking, for example, at "Justice Sunday," a 2005 meeting organized by some of the more extremist groups associated with the religious right, including Focus on the Family. Thus, in the first decade of the twenty-first century, there are two political parties each appealing to their respective bases, but the base of one is much further from the center than the base of the other. The culture war being fought by partisans and ideologues continues because conservatives and Republicans want to see it continue.

In his widely read book *What's the Matter with Kansas?* Tom Frank suggests one such reason for this conclusion: the primary objective of

Republicans, he argues, is to pass legislation beneficial to the rich and powerful interests that support them.[17] Since there is no "natural" majority for such policies, premised as they are on rewarding the few at the expense of the many, Republicans need the culture war to keep the support of voters whose economic interests suffer when Republicans come to power. Frank's argument is weakened by his failure to consider that conservative voters may have legitimate complaints about how liberals have treated the views of people of faith, but his basic proposition is nonetheless true. Even if—especially if—one believes that the election of 2004 hinged on moral values, it is striking that the first acts of the new Republican Congress involved bankruptcy reform and Social Security privatization, only to shift back once again to the issues such as flag burning and gay marriage as a new election cycle approached. The only real complaint one can make about Frank's analysis is that it is too obvious; Republicans act as if his book is not a criticism of them but rather a guidebook for their political strategy.

There are additional reasons why the fate of the Republicans has become intertwined with the fate of the culture war. These days Republicans are far more likely to approach politics as it were war in the first place. Their troops tend to be highly disciplined. They stay on message. They are exceptionally adept at negative campaigning and are able to make their charges against their opponents stick. They use control over government to promote their party and ideology to a degree unprecedented in recent American politics. The astonishing political success of Republicans is premised upon mobilizing high levels of anger within the electorate—one reason why conservatives tend so often to see themselves as victims of liberal elitists, even when liberals have relatively little political power. In the 2004 election, Democrats who voted for John Kerry could correctly identify the positions of their candidate better than Republicans who voted for George W. Bush, a clear indication that one side was motivated more by policy and the other by intangibles such as character.[18] A politics of passion fits the current conservative mood in America far more properly than a politics of restraint, and rarely in American politics have we seen a politics as passionate as that of red-state legislators convinced that moral decadence is running rampant in the United States.

Conservatives may well have reason for their passion. It is impossible to understand the form the American culture war has taken without grasping its central paradox: America has moved to the right politically at the same time it has moved to the left culturally. Some conservatives, such as Gertrude Himmelfarb, believe that if the culture war seems over, it is essentially because the left has won; America, she writes, is confronting "the collapse of ethical principles and habits, the loss of respect for authorities and institutions, the breakdown of the family, the decline of civility, the vulgarization of high culture, and the degradation of popular culture."[19] One need not agree with her strong language to conclude that her basic point has some validity: on affirmative action, gay marriage, stem cell research, and Terri Schiavo, American public opinion has shifted in the direction of allowing individuals some say in their own morality rather than relying on traditional deference to authority.[20] As conservatives rightly insist, the values of the 1960s have permeated American society; even conservatism would not be the strong national movement it has become without a libertarian component insisting on the importance of individual choice.

Yet if American culture has moved left, American politics have moved right. The presidency, both houses of Congress, and the Supreme Court have conservative majorities. Liberalism has become a term so widely disliked in the United States that even liberals seek other adjectives to describe their views. Especially since the 1994 election, when their party gained a significant number of seats in the House of Representatives, the United States has witnessed the emergence of a new Republican era.[21] And the Republicans are not only in the majority, they are led by politicians far more conservative than Barry Goldwater or Ronald Reagan. So far to the right has the tone of the Republican Party shifted that even as conservative a man as Supreme Court Justice Anthony Kennedy can be attacked by House majority leader Tom DeLay as if he were a liberal activist. Since Goldwater's decisive defeat in 1964, the Republican Party has not only become more conservative, but, defying once widely held assumptions about political success in America, it has come to dominate Washington and a very high number of state governments at the same time. As political success goes, it is difficult to imagine a greater one than this.

The fact that conservatives control politics but not the culture fuels the anger of those who are convinced that their will is being thwarted. Surely, they believe, someone or something must be standing in the way of their inability to stop what they view as horrendous crimes, such as what they called the "murder" of Terri Schiavo. Historically predisposed to conspiracy theorizing, adherents of the hard right in American politics blame everyone they can for their plight: liberals, judges, bureaucrats, the media.[22] Their inability to use their political power to lower the abortion and divorce rates, instill a sense of obedience and respect for authority among teenagers, and urge courts and legislatures to give special recognition to Christianity's prominent role in American religious life creates among them a perpetual outrage machine. Gripped by a conviction that politics can and should change human hearts, they have limitless battles in front of them; ending the culture war would mean that they could relax their vigilance—and that, in the face of what they view as widespread moral degradation, is not something they are prepared to do.

Ironically, however, the same gap between political success and cultural failure that fuels the culture war could also at some point contribute to its end. The more that conservatives dominate American politics, the harder it becomes to make the argument that America's moral problems are caused by liberals. Should religious conservatives finally get their political reward in the form of new justices to the Supreme Court, their control over the American political system would be complete. Yet not even complete control over the political system is likely to transform American culture back to a period when clergy had unquestioned authority, husbands worked and wives stayed home, divorce was infrequent, stepchildren were rare, and gambling was confined to one state and pornography to seedy downtowns. As they reflect on their failure to use their political weight to bring out the cultural transformation they so strongly desire, conservative religious believers may discover that there is another option available to them other than a politics of anger and paranoia: they can put their religious faith on a higher pedestal than their political activism.

Between roughly the 1920s and 1970s, conservative Christians did not play an active role in politics, convinced that matters as important to them as spirituality and faith would only be compromised by blending with matters of campaign strategy and logrolling. Perhaps they were correct in their assessment. It is not only that politics may, in the end, have little impact on the human heart. It is also that politics offers endless temptation for corruption and sin, as witnessed by the close ties to casino gambling associated with believers such as Ralph Reed or the financial contributions to the Republican Party from corporations such as AT&T or Rupert Murdoch's Fox News, which are invested in providing pornography. It is not far-fetched to suggest that further revelations among these lines could convince large numbers of evangelicals that Roger Williams, who warned of the extent to which the purity of faith could be corrupted by the temptations of power, knew what he was talking about.

The longer politically conservative leaders remain in power without having any significant impact on transforming American culture (except, in my decidedly liberal opinion, to coarsen it even further), the greater the likelihood that the base of conservative voters who provide their support will shrink. Would such a development help close the gap between the culture war the elites are fighting and the absence of a culture war in American opinion more generally? There are, in my view, two developments required to bring the culture war to an end. One of them has already happened; the other remains undetermined.

The one that has already happened is that Democrats have by and large engaged in a new tactic with respect to the culture war: they have called a truce. Not only are Democratic politicians scurrying to the center of the political spectrum—a wise move given how politically conservative the United States has become—but the days in which liberals relied on courts to ensure the victory of programs wildly out of touch with American democratic sentiment seem long past. Indeed, liberals have taken to questioning whether judicial review itself ought to be given a place in a democratic society that should rely more often on the will of the people themselves.[23] (As if on cue, the Republicans seem determined to take a reverse stance by promoting judicial activists of their own, including those who would overturn duly passed legislation regulating the economy on the grounds that such laws violate property rights; the Federalist Society and Judge Janice Rogers Brown are as undemocratic on the right as Ronald Dworkin has been on the left.) Liberal activists still exist in the Democratic Party, and much financial support and campaign energy continues to come from those who support a woman's right to choose or laws and court decisions that would allow for gay marriage. But the trends within the party either discourage firebrands on the left or, as seems to be the case with Howard Dean, temper them by subjecting them to the requirements of fundraising and party organization. Democrats, moreover, know that their political fortunes improve to the extent that elections focus on economic issues or such pre-culture-war concerns as Social Security. In the Terri Schiavo affair, Democrats opted for silence, their best option under the circumstances.

The other development that might bring the politics of the culture war to an end still awaits its denouement: conservatives motivated by passionate anger about the moral decline of their country will need to become more introspective. Moral decline has many causes, and surely among them would be the one conservative Christians are likely to put first: the warped priorities of the entertainment industry and the (frequently liberal) politicians to which that industry disproportionately contributes. The quality of life in the United States is hardly improved by Whoopi Goldberg's scatological comments on the president's name. It is improved when figures like William Bennett, Joseph Lieberman, and Delores Tucker join together to oppose the filth that passes for popular entertainment in America.

But while Hollywood is certainly entitled to its share of blame for what children watch and do, not far behind, and perhaps even ahead, are the choices made by individuals themselves. One of the more fascinating factoids to emerge from the 2004 election was that states that voted strongly Republican, such as Texas and Oklahoma, had far higher rates of divorce than those that voted for Democrats, such as Massachusetts and Connecticut. Before blaming liberals in California or New England for the teenage promiscuity and out-of-wedlock births they see in their local communities, Americans in the red states might consider that politics, even conservative politics, cannot help them if their marriages are unhappy, their children rebellious, and their willpower weak. Sometimes people have to look inward as well as outward. Those who have been born again in Christ ought to be among the first to understand this very basic truth.

The Religious Factor

While considerable attention has been paid to the way changes in American politics fuel America's ongoing culture war, less attention has been paid to what has been taking place in American religion. The notion that the United States is gripped by a culture war assumes that Americans are increasingly divided between those for whom religion, especially conservative religion, has become the most powerful force in their lives and those whose outlook on the world is primarily secular. Yet while there is some truth to this picture, it is also a drastically oversimplified view of what is really happening in the fascinating tumult that constitutes contemporary religious practice in the United States.

Conservative churches are certainly growing, at least among Protestants; no one doubts that evangelicals are gaining at the expense of such mainline religions as the Episcopal Church.[24] (It does not help the Episcopal Church's future prospects that its members are so divided on issues such as homosexuality.) As they contemplate statistics demonstrating the appeal of Pentecostal and evangelical insistence on strict biblical literalism and the ubiquity of sin, scholars of American religion are wont to conclude that strict churches—strongly committed to doctrine, traditionalist in their view of gender roles, and insistent on clerical authority—are attracting more Americans because they stand in such sharp contrast to the more questioning and hesitant practices associated with mainline faiths.[25] The culture war, from this perspective, is fueled by the desires of ever larger numbers of Americans to turn their backs on secularism and liberalism in favor of something resembling the old-time religion.

In religion as in politics, however, the conventional wisdom is not our best guide. For one thing, the story of the evangelical revival contains some obvious exceptions. Although African Americans make up roughly 12 percent of the American population, they constitute a higher proportion of the American Protestant population. And while large numbers of African Americans are conservative in their religious beliefs—support for gay rights is not exactly very high in most of America's inner cities—they remain overwhelmingly liberal in their political views. Despite determined efforts to make inroads, Republicans have not been successful at persuading African Americans to vote for them. Any conclusion that the rise of conservative religion means greater support for conservative politics, in short, must immediately be discounted by a factor of roughly 20 percent, a reasonable estimate of the proportion of the evangelical Protestant population that is African American. And that discount does not include a small, but still significant, number of white evangelicals who, for political or theological reasons, still tend to vote Democratic.

In addition, unlike white evangelicals, America's other religious communities have not shown a corresponding conservative shift. For the sake of interreligious harmony, it may be helpful to conclude that Jews are undergoing religious transformations similar to those being experienced by Protestants, but the fact is that they are not. Among Jews there has been no significant shift away from their political liberalism.[26] And it is actually Conservative Judaism, squeezed between Reform on its left and Orthodox Judaism on its right, that is declining.[27] Nor has there been a sharp shift to the right among Catholics. It is true that Catholics are now more likely to vote for Republicans than they were when John F. Kennedy ran for president in 1960. But this has more to do with rising socioeconomic status among Catholics than it does with a religious revival. There has been a small shift toward more conservative forms of Catholicism in the United States, but it has been overwhelmed by the tendency of American Catholics to make up their own minds about the kind of Catholics they want to be. By huge majorities they believe they can be good Catholics without attending church on Sunday (76 percent), obeying the Church's teachings on birth control (71 percent), or remarrying after divorce without seeking an annulment (64 percent).[28] And, as it happens, younger American Catholics are even more inclined to reinvent their religion to suit their personal views and needs than their parents and grandparents are.[29] This trend is matched in other religious communities, which have seen young people insist on the importance of faith in their lives even as they manifest little knowledge of the details of the faiths to which they adhere.[30]

If these reports are accurate, the presumed religious revival occurring in the United States is confined to pretty much one, albeit large, religious group. Yet a closer look at the data suggests that even this conclusion is not completely accurate. Conservative churches may be growing, but it is not true that many so-called conservative churches are really conservative, at least as that term is traditionally understood. Those who believe that strict teachings explain why Americans are attracted to conservative churches tend to focus on quantitative data that show strong upturns in membership among Pentecostal and evangelical denominations and congregations. But qualitative data—case studies of those denominations and congregations themselves—suggest that their teachings are not as strict as they are often assumed to be.[31]

As the historian George Marsden correctly points out, conservative Protestantism experienced a revival in twentieth-century American life due to the influence of thinkers such as J. Gresham Machen, an intellectually serious Reformed theologian intent on developing a Christian alternative to secularism and modernism.[32] Those flocking to America's megachurches, however, are not doing so for reasons that have much, if anything, to do with theology, Reformed or otherwise. Fully aware of this, megachurch leaders—who in any case lack substantial authority in a religious movement that distrusts hierarchy and considers itself a priesthood of all believers—play down the importance of doctrine in their sermons and small groups. They create a welcoming atmosphere in which people who might be turned off by religious certainty will experience the warmth and sense of community of a loving environment. When I asked the founding pastor of a rapidly growing church outside Cincinnati if he could summarize his teachings, he responded by saying, "Love, love, love, love, truth." Matters of doctrine—the strict teachings long identified with Protestantism's history—were important to him, but only secondarily. He pays more attention to getting the music right—and the music, lest there be any doubt, is rock music played on electronic instruments, not Bach played on an organ—than he does to clarifying the differences between premillennial and postmillennial Christianity.

Along similar lines, the popular idea that Americans are attracted to conservative Christianity because they are traditionalists at heart who want to return to the morality prominent in the United States before the 1960s runs into the complication that evangelical Protestantism is anything but traditional in its outlook on the world. If I had to invent a term that meant the exact opposite of "traditional," I would use the phrase that evangelicals apply to themselves: "born again." To be traditional is to be born into a world shaped by one's parents and grandparents and to feel an obligation to pass that world on unchanged to one's children and grandchildren. Such traditionalism is important to many American religious believers, primarily to Jews, who frequently assign a higher importance to honoring the traditions than to believing in God. But for evangelicals, authenticity of belief is primary and adherence to tradition secondary. If the religion an individual inherits from his family and community worships Jesus in the wrong way, then one must break with tradition in favor of right worship and devotion.

It is because evangelicals assign a relatively low value to tradition that their faith has grown so rapidly in the decidedly nontraditional environment of American culture. Committed to spreading the good news of the Gospel, evangelicals rely on every innovative twist in the culture to reach those in need of salvation, not only the highly innovative megachurch but the latest developments in media, information technology, and mass entertainment. If members need day care for their children while engaged in frightfully long commutes from their exurb to downtown Atlanta or Minneapolis, the church will provide it. If not displaying a cross will bring in more of the unchurched, the cross will not be displayed. If young people want preachers that can speak their slang, preachers will be trained who can speak their slang. If women need to work to support the family's lifestyle, they will not be told from the pulpit that their Christian duty requires that they stay at home to be full-time mothers. If best-selling authors want to introduce believers to old-fashioned ideas about the end times, they do so through the medium of science fiction. Of course, there are numerous conservative Christians in America who find in their faith a way to reject modern America's narcissistic quest for individual empowerment and satisfaction, but there are also great numbers of conservative Christians who discover through their faith a way to cope with the world around them. Those who know about J. Gresham Machen's long struggle against modernity—and few conservative Christians do—would not find in it many lessons that would apply to them.

Hardly traditional in the usual sense of the term and more interested in a God who loves them than in one who hectors them about their false ideas, America's religious believers, including a significant number of those who would describe themselves as conservative Christians, are not consumed by their own sinfulness and wallowing in self-doubt. Theirs is a confident religion, one that is upbeat about human potential and intent on finding positive things to say to those flocking into churches for Sunday services. It is not that sin has disappeared so much as it has been transformed. Not that long ago, Christians were told that God wanted them to avoid making themselves too attractive, but now evangelical and Pentecostal parachurch movements emphasize the importance of beautification, while diet books outsell those about the Bible at Christian bookstores.[33] The line between religious faith and self-help is increasingly hard to draw, a point that has been brought to our attention with great insight by James Davison Hunter.[34] As Hunter rightly observes, there is much to deplore in a religion that has lost touch with its historic mission of reminding us of our duties to God and the grievous consequences that follow from breaking them. But a faith that overlaps with therapy does have one redeeming feature. People have throughout time killed for their beliefs; they are unlikely to do so for their feelings.

Before moral values were held to determine the results of the 2004 presidential election, religion was being cited as the major reason why Americans divided themselves into political parties the way they did. "The single greatest divide in American politics," Michael Barone wrote after the 2000 election, "is that the Bush coalition consists of people who are religious and respect traditional morality while the Gore coalition consists of people who are not traditionally religious and favor a more relativistic morality."[35] Barone's is the conventional wisdom, and, as such, it is not quite right. It would be more accurate to say that churchgoers—or, to be even more precise, those who tell pollsters that they attend church regularly (which may not be the same as those who actually do)—are more likely to vote Republican than Democratic, but few who are attracted to either political party are exclusively traditionalists on the one hand or relativists on the other.[36] Everyone in America, as I wrote in *One Nation, After All*, is both a traditionalist and a modernist, religious believers included. Americans long for the well-tested practices of the past as they embrace the potential held out by the future.

And the Secular Factor As Well

If religious believers in America, even those who identify themselves as conservative Christians, bear little resemblance to the fundamentalists caricatured in "Inherit the Wind," secularists are not quite the Clarence-Darrow-like determined opponents of all things spiritual they are frequently made out to be. For all the talk of a religious revival in the United States, the proportion of Americans who identified themselves to pollsters as having no religious preference doubled, from 7 to 14 percent, over the course of the 1990s.[37] It is, so to speak, an article of faith among the leaders of the religious right than America is turning away from its religious roots in favor of a reign of secular humanism in which nonbelief will become the ruling ideology. The increasing numbers of Americans who fail to identify themselves as religious would seem to support that claim; there are, in all likelihood, more Americans who make religion a secondary force in their lives today than at any time in American history. No wonder that a Jerry Falwell or Pat Robertson is convinced that Christians are a persecuted minority facing a determined foe, hostile to religion in all its forms and to conservative Christianity with special vehemence.

Yet any characterization of the United States as entering into a period of rampant secularism is as inaccurate as any that portrays the emergence of a new great awakening. For one thing, the best available explanation of the increase in those who do not identify themselves as religious concludes that they do so not for reasons of unbelief but as a reaction against self-identified Christians; there has been no comparable change, for example, in the number of Americans who say they believe in God.[38] Other evidence suggests that large numbers of Americans who do not consider themselves religious do consider themselves spiritual in one way or another; exiting from religion, in other words, does not imply entering into atheism.[39] Just as American religious believers cannot escape the modernism of American culture, America's nonbelievers cannot escape the religious coloration of American culture. America has a culture in which belief and nonbelief continually blend in ever newer syntheses that resemble neither the old-time religion nor latter-day secular humanism.

There are, to be sure, political activists committed to erecting a sharp barrier between church and state in the United States (just as there are others equally determined to break that barrier down). Americans United for Separation of Church and State and the American Civil Liberties Union can be considered active participants in the American culture war.

They have strong views about the relatively small role that religion should play in American public life, rely on the courts more than on democratically elected legislatures to enforce their views, and raise funds and energize their base by insisting on the harm their opponents, primarily conservative Christians, will cause if their power is not checked. To the extent that their objectives are realized, the battle between a more secular and a more religious understanding of American public life would be tilted in favor of the former.

Back in the days when the culture war really did have two sides, advocates for strict separation of church and state were an important component of one side. For roughly a decade and a half, from the 1970s until the mid-1980s, the Supreme Court came as close as it ever has to the effective disestablishment of religion in American public life, as it struck down the practice of displaying nativity scenes in public places or inviting clergy to speak at public high school graduations.[40] Those decisions fueled the American culture war, and for one simple reason: questions involving the proper boundaries between faith and politics really are nonnegotiable. If religious symbols are not allowed in the public square, believers cannot find in public places reaffirmations of their faith; but if religious symbols are allowed in the public square, nonbelievers are treated as less than fully equal to believers. However the courts resolve these questions, someone will feel aggrieved, and when the Supreme Court was in its strict separationist phase, there is no doubt that believers both felt victimized and had justification for feeling that way.

But without any formal declaration, the Court has moved away from strict separationism in some of its more recent decisions, starting with its willingness to allow evangelicals to benefit from student fees at a public university.[41] There is, moreover, little chance that the current Supreme Court, even without any new members, would revisit the era of William Brennan and Thurgood Marshall, and should President Bush get to choose new members, the Court is likely to shift even further in the direction of accommodating religion in public places. Time will tell whether the Court, which once established itself too far to the left on these issues, will find itself too far to the right. But over the course of American history, constitutional jurisprudence with respect to church-state issues has been too confused and contradictory to support any side in the culture war. However, it is especially true for the conservative side: any suggestion that secular humanists run the country in ways that oppress religious believers—the staple of rhetoric coming from the religious right these days—is likely to be laughed out of court at a time when the balance on church-state issues is shifting back in the direction of respecting religious practice.

One of the most frustrating features of debates about the culture war is the lack of a comparison point. Saying we have a culture war is like saying that someone has a fever. Not much information is provided by such a diagnosis unless we know whether the fever is higher than the one this person usually gets when sick or, even if it is, whether it is high enough to cause a serious crisis in the person's health.

One such standard would evaluate the seriousness of our contemporary culture war in comparison to those arising earlier in our history. By that standard, America's current culture war is weak indeed; the level of violence it has engendered is nowhere near what the United States experienced during the Civil War or even during the 1960s, when, to borrow from the title of one of James Hunter's books, the shooting really did begin.[42] And even the violence that did exist a decade or so ago, when Hunter wrote his book, has subsided; thankfully, not that many abortion providers have been killed in recent years.

The question of religion's role in American public life suggests a second point of comparison that helps put the culture war in perspective: how is the United States doing in relation to similar countries, such as those in Western Europe? And here again the evidence suggests that compared to their cultural conflicts, the American culture war is a rather tame affair.

To cite the most visible example, America's culture war, whatever it does entail, does not involve hostility toward and fear of Islam; headscarves just do not arouse the same anger in New York City that they do in Paris. When French intellectuals defend the ban on headscarves, moreover, they do so by claiming that they are not anti-Muslim but opposed to any conspicuous displays of religion, thereby opening up a new chapter in a two-century-old war between religion and the Enlightenment. This, too, is a war our country has skipped. Unlike France, the United States has never had a clerical or an anticlerical tradition, which helps explain why those who push for the teaching of creationism claim (implausibly, in my view) that they are doing so in the name of science.

Nor is the culture war anything like what the Germans called the *Kulturkampf*: their bitter struggle between Protestants and Catholics. While Americans had such a struggle in the nineteenth century—our first culture war, so to speak—Protestants and Catholics in the United States have dropped their mutual hostility. When the Catholic Church experienced its sexual abuse crisis, conservative Protestants responded with sympathy, not with attacks on Vatican decadence. If you want to see societies in which religion really does play a divisive role in public life, look across the Atlantic.

The Founders actually established a pretty good way to resolve the kind of sectarian conflicts over religion that plagued Europe, and that was by guaranteeing its free exercise. Their wisdom has worked wonders, and as a result Americans have been spared the bitter, unending conflicts that so many other societies have faced. Whatever conflicts remain over these issues, they pale in significance to those that have been resolved.

After the Culture War

In the seven years since *One Nation, After All* was published, I have watched with obvious interest as the book's findings have gone in and out of fashion. Soon after the book appeared, Republicans tried to impeach and convict Bill Clinton, and their failure to do the latter suggested that Americans were indeed as nonjudgmental as I had portrayed them in the book. Then came the two elections of 2000 and 2004, and the very map of the United States seemed to demonstrate how wrong I was; how could Americans be "one nation, after all" and still be divided into red states and blue states? But as soon as it was established that the culture war was alive and well, the Republican Party seemed to overreach again in the Schiavo affair, much as it had during the impeachment imbroglio, leading large numbers of Americans to worry that the country was headed in the wrong direction and that appointing conservative judges over Democratic objections was not the best way to set it on the right track. Having changed so frequently, the mood may change again: who knows if the next chapter in this ever unfolding story will be one in which moral values become the real factor in the election of 2008 that they were not in 2004?

No one can deny that issues that touch on fundamental questions of human purpose, moral obligation, and the nature of the divinity are a challenge for a political system that requires a certain level of consensus and stability in order to operate. Clearly, something has changed in American politics since the days when tariffs, antitrust legislation, and nuclear power plants dominated the headlines. American democracy is not especially well prepared to handle ideological passion, all-or-nothing extremism, and apocalyptic scenarios. But as long as politicians feel a need to rouse their base, media outlets look for the most dramatic and emotional stories, and single-issue groups lobby as hard for their agenda as they ignore considerations of the common good, the culture war will be with us in one form or another.

Yet while prediction in politics is always hazardous, I hold fast to the ones I made in 1998. Americans, I believe, were on the right track when they reacted without enthusiasm to partisan efforts to impeach a duly elected president of the United States, no matter how offensive his (essentially private) conduct. Rather than rely on such an extreme measure to punish Mr. Clinton for his behavior, many of them did what in a democracy is the proper thing to do: they voted against his party in the next election. And there, or so I believe, matters would have stood had the 2000 election offered a decisive outcome. Either we would have concluded that Americans simply did not want to focus on stained dresses and various definitions of sex, or we would have viewed Clinton's escapades as an indication of moral decay and expressed our hopes that a new president and party would avoid such excesses.

But, as we all know, there was no such resolution in the election of 2000. From the standpoint of healing the wounds that had been inflicted on American politics by the Clinton impeachment, nothing could have been more counterproductive than an electoral stalemate. Given the closeness of the vote, bitterness on the part of the loser was inevitable. To his eternal credit, Vice President Gore handled his defeat with dignity, but this did not stop a sense of outrage from manifesting itself on the left end of the political spectrum in, for example, the films of Michael Moore. One cannot know, of course, what might have happened had the tables been reversed and the Democrats proclaimed the victory, but it is hard to imagine that there would not have been equal, if not higher, levels of bitterness on the right. Indeed, a pronounced bitterness could be detected among some conservatives even though Mr. Bush was declared the winner. A clear victor from either party would have been a better outcome for democratic stability in 2000 than a virtual tie. The lack of a clear winner all but guaranteed that the culture war would go on: political systems do not like indecisive elections, whereas ideological crusades thrive on them.

If the election of 2000 gave unexpected new energy to the culture war, the tragedy unleashed on September 11, 2001, seemed to stop it in its tracks. Some pundits—I was one of them—took to print to suggest that battles over gay rights or stem cells were going to seem pretty puny when Americans were in the midst of a real war against real enemies; if Osama bin Laden did not care whether you were gay or straight, why should your coworkers?[43] This was not one of my predictions that turned out to be correct. To be sure, there was a period in the immediate aftermath of September 11 when Americans of all persuasions came together to hang flags and support the first responders; the sense of unity that emerged after September 11 was not only noticeable but welcome by just about all. As horrendous as that day was, for one brief shining moment the culture war was nowhere to be found. There was some fluttering along those lines, of course, as some blamed America for provoking the attacks against it and others denounced them for their lack of patriotism, but these moments paled in the face of bipartisan resolve to do whatever it took to right the wrong.

Within a breathtakingly short period of time, the unity and sense of common purpose so visible after September 11 disappeared. Since historians will be debating the question of why for a long time to come, I certainly cannot offer a definitive explanation here. But there is little doubt in my mind that the culture war came back because the party in power when the attack happened, the Republican Party, was simply not prepared to let it go. The script outlining how the Republicans could become the dominant party had already been written, and neither George W. Bush, Karl Rove, nor the very large number of extremely conservative Republicans in Congress were going to work together with Democrats and liberals when attacking them was so crucial to their long-term political plans.

It did not matter that Democrats voted overwhelmingly for authorizing the war against Iraq, even if, as it turns out, reasons existed to question the administration's rationale for going to war; Republicans would hint that they were disloyal in any case. Nor did it matter that Democrats and liberals had already signaled their intention to put culture war issues on the back burner; the moment they did so, Republicans could then accuse them of flip-flopping. The only thing that mattered was that the president's reelection was dependent upon mobilizing the four million evangelical votes that Mr. Rove believed stayed home in 2004. If invoking the culture of life, nominating ultraconservative judges, and holding fast to an incoherent decision on stem cells would bring out those voters, that is what the party and its leadership would do.

Of course, the Republicans were helped in these efforts by liberals with their own stake in the culture war. There was, I believe, no compelling reason for the Supreme Judicial Court of Massachusetts to issue such a sweeping position on gay marriage before the country had had a deep debate on the issue. And as the initial success of Howard Dean in the 2004 primaries suggested, the left wing of the Democratic Party was still alive and well and determined to shape the party in the direction it favored. Bill Clinton and Al Gore had shifted the party more to the center, but anger at George W. Bush was pushing it back to the left.

Still, President Bush, who for a few months after September 11 rose above politics to become the national leader Americans craved, bears the ultimate responsibility for ultimately choosing a strategy of division and discord to promote an ideologically driven, partisan agenda. History will, I am certain, judge him a failure for not seizing the moment to become the unifying figure America so desperately needed at that time. And even if he had been inclined to do so, Mr. Bush would have faced a revolt from ideological zealots in his party far to his right. The influence of the Christian right on Republican politics is now so strong that even a politician known as a "maverick," Arizona senator John McCain, has to appeal to right-wing leaders such as Jerry Falwell, whom he once had denounced as intolerant.

Yet history has its ironies, and one of them may be that although Mr. Bush refused to abandon the culture war, the culture war abandoned him. Only time will tell if the Republicans overreached in the Terri Schiavo case and in their determination not only to appoint the most conservative judges they can to America's courts but in their willingness to break long-standing traditions to do so. But if they did overreach—and early signs suggest that this is exactly what they have done—it will be because Americans want from their leaders the same kind of moderation and balance they desire in themselves. We are not a nation of zealots determined to make enemies of each other. We are instead a society that, faced with crises in the past, eventually found ways to come together in defense of our common heritage. That sense of unity has been delayed in the wake of September 11, but it still may emerge. If it does, it will be in spite of the efforts made by some of our most powerful politicians at the moment, not because of them.

Notes

1. ABC News, "Poll: No Role for Government in Schiavo Case," March 21, 2005 (abcnews.go.com/Politics/PollVault/story?id=599622&page=1).

2. Alan Wolfe, *One Nation, After All: What Middle Class Americans Really Think about God, Country, Family, Racism, Welfare, Immigration, Homosexuality, Work, the Right, the Left, and Each Other* (New York: Viking Penguin, 1998).

3. Cited in D. Sunshine Hillygus and Todd G. Shields, "Moral Issues and Voter Decision Making in the 2004 Presidential Election," *PS: Political Science and Politics* 38 (April 2005): 201–11.

4. On the 20 percent figure, see Frederick Turner, "The Double Citizen: Religious and Secular," *Society* 42 (May-June 2005): 14. The quote from the member of the President's Council on Bioethics is from Peter Augustine Lawler, "Virtue Voters," *Society* 42 (May–June 2005): 23.

5. Hillygus and Shields, "Moral Issues," p. 207.

6. Kevin Philips, *The Emerging Republican Majority* (New Rochelle, N.Y.: Arlington House, 1969).

7. Wolfe, *One Nation, After All*.

8. E. J. Dionne, *Why Americans Hate Politics* (New York: Simon and Schuster, 1991).

9. Morris P. Fiorina, Samuel J. Abrams, and Jeremy C. Pope, *Culture Wars: The Myth of a Polarized America* (New York: Pearson Longman, 2005), pp. 34–54.

10. Gregory B. Lewis, "Same-Sex Marriage and the 2004 Presidential Election," *PS: Political Science and Politics* 38 (April 2005): 195–99.

11. Fiorina, Abrams, and Pope, *Culture Wars*, p. 64.

12. John R. Hibbing and Elizabeth Theiss-Morse, *Stealth Democracy: Americans' Beliefs about How Government Should Work* (New York: Cambridge University Press, 2002).

13. This theme runs throughout Wolfe, *One Nation, After All.*

14. Jim Wallis, *God's Politics: Why the Right Gets It Wrong and the Left Doesn't Get It* (San Francisco: Harpers, 2005).

15. See the still relevant Ethan Bronner, *Battle for Justice: How the Bork Nomination Shook America* (New York: Norton, 1989).

16. Ronald Dworkin, *A Matter of Principle* (Harvard University Press, 1985), pp. 196–97.

17. Thomas Frank, *What's the Matter with Kansas? How Conservatives Won the Heart of America* (New York: Metropolitan Books, 2004).

18. Program on International Policy Attitudes, Knowledge Networks Poll, "The Separate Realities of Bush and Kerry Supporters," October 21, 2004 (www. pipa.org/OnlineReports/Pres_Election_04/Report10_21_04.pdf).

19. Gertrude Himmelfarb, *One Nation, Two Cultures* (New York: Knopf, 1999), p. 20.

20. See Alan Wolfe, *Moral Freedom: The Search for Virtue in a World of Choice* (New York: Norton, 2001).

21. Alan I. Abramowitz, "The End of the Democratic Era? 1994 and the Future of Congressional Election Research," *Political Research Quarterly* 48 (December 1995): 873–89.

22. Richard Hofstadter, *The Paranoid Style in American Politics and Other Essays* (New York: Knopf, 1964), pp. 3–40.

23. See Larry Kramer, *The People Themselves: Popular Constitutionalism and Judicial Review* (New York: Oxford University Press, 2004).

24. On mainline decline and evangelical growth, see David A. Roozen, "Denominations Grow as Individuals Join Congregations," in *Church and Denominational Growth: What Does (and Does Not) Cause Growth or Decline*, edited by David A. Roozen and C. Kirk Hadaway (Nashville: Abingdon Press, 1993), pp. 16–17.

25. See Dean M. Kelley, *Why Conservative Churches Are Growing* (New York: Harper and Row, 1972), and Rodney Stark and Roger Finke, *Acts of Faith: Explaining the Human Side of Religion* (Berkeley and Los Angeles: University of California Press, 2000), p. 276.

26. Kenneth D. Wald, "The Probable Persistence of American Jewish Liberalism," in *Religion as a Public Good: Jews and Other Americans on Religion in the Public Square*, edited by Alan Mittleman (Lanham, Md: Rowman and Littlefield, 2003), pp. 65–90.

27. Jack Wertheimer, ed., *Jews in the Center: Conservative Synagogues and Their Members* (Rutgers University Press, 2000).

28. William V. D'Antonio and others, *American Catholics: Gender, Generation, and Commitment* (Walnut Creek, Calif: AltaMira, 2001), p. 43.

29. Dean R. Hoge and others, *Young American Catholics: Religion in the Culture of Choice* (University of Notre Dame Press, 2001).

30. Christian Smith and Melinda Lundquist Denton, *Soul Searching: The Religious and Spiritual Lives of American Teenagers* (New York: Oxford University Press, 2005).

31. The next four paragraphs summarize some of the arguments in Alan Wolfe, *The Transformation of American Religion: How We Actually Live Our Faith* (New York: Free Press, 2003).

32. George M. Marsden, *Fundamentalism and American Culture: The Shaping of Twentieth Century Evangelicalism 1870–1925* (New York: Oxford University Press, 1980).

33. R. Marie Griffith, *Born-Again Bodies: Flesh and Spirit in American Christianity* (Berkeley and Los Angeles: University of California Press, 2004).

34. James Davison Hunter, *The Death of Character: Moral Education in an Age without Good or Evil* (New York: Basic Books, 2000).

35. Cited in Adrian Woolridge, "As Labor Lost Ideology, U.S. Parties Found It," *New York Times*, July 22, 2001, section 4, p. 4.

36. For a discussion about the accuracy of self-reported church attendance, see C. Kirk Hadaway, Penny Marler, and Mark Chaves, "Over-reporting Church Attendance in America: Evidence that Demands the Same Verdict," *American Sociological Review* 63 (February 1998): 122–30.

37. Michael Hout and Claude S. Fischer, "Why Americans Have No Religious Preference: Politics and Generations," *American Sociological Review* 67 (April 2002): 165–90.

38. Ibid.

39. Robert C. Fuller, *Spiritual but Not Religious: Understanding Unchurched America* (New York: Oxford University Press, 2001).

40. *County of Allegheny* v. *American Civil Liberties Union, Greater Pittsburgh Chapter*, 492 U.S. 573 (1989); *Lee* v. *Weisman*, 505 U.S. 577 (1992).

41. *Rosenberger* v. *Rector and Visitors of University of Virginia*, 515 U.S. 819 (1995).

42. James Davison Hunter, *Before the Shooting Begins: Searching for Democracy in America's Culture War* (New York: Free Press, 1994).

43. Alan Wolfe, "The Home Front: American Society Responds to the New War," in *How Did This Happen? Terrorism and the New War*, edited by James F. Hoge Jr. and Gideon Rose (New York: Public Affairs Press, 2001), pp. 283–93.

COMMENT

THE OTHER CULTURE WAR

GERTRUDE HIMMELFARB

THE CULTURE WAR has taken an interesting turn. Combatants on both sides are declaring victory and, in doing so, pronouncing the culture war over and done with. This is especially odd at a time when the Schiavo case, the Supreme Court nominations, abortion, and gay marriage have inflamed tempers and exacerbated the divisions between liberals and conservatives, Democrats and Republicans. Before that there was the election of 2004 that produced the map demarcating "red" and "blue" America as cultural as well as political entities. And before that there were the evangelicals who brought the religious-secular divide into the public arena and made it a major subject of contention. Yet it is now, in this overheated climate, that liberals and conservatives seem to be agreeing on one thing and one thing only: that the culture war is over.

Indeed, for some—for Alan Wolfe, most notably—there never was a war, at least not among the "suburban middle class Americans" who were the subject of his *One Nation, After All*; it was primarily "intellectuals" who were fighting that war.[1] (In his present essay, the war exists mainly in the "minds of journalists and political activists.") Most Americans, ordinary Americans, he then argued, are not involved in a culture war because, unlike these intellectuals, they are "nonjudgmental," share much the same moral values, and conduct their lives in very similar ways. This is still his view of the American public, although he now modifies his conclusion slightly, perhaps in view of all the controversies that have had such high political visibility. He no longer claims that there is no culture war, rather that it is "on its last legs." Those who persist in fighting it, he predicts, "are likely to find themselves on the sideline in America's political future."

Some conservatives, who were once on the front lines in the culture war and do not welcome being shunted to the sideline, are now pleased to report that the war is over (or almost over) because they are winning it. It is in this spirit that administration spokesmen took the overwhelmingly patriotic response to September 11 as evidence of the "soundness," of the moral and social health of the American people. Others have come to the same conclusion for different reasons. They cite the social indicators showing a decline in the incidence of crime, violence, abortion, drug use, divorce, and out-of-wedlock births among adults and, more important, among young people. Andrew Sullivan, in the London *Times,* takes these as a refutation of American "cultural declinists" and as an object lesson for the British, who are urged to learn from American experiences—from American conservatives in particular, who sponsored policies that reduced crime and domestic violence, discouraged welfare dependency, deterred abortions and teenage pregnancy, and removed the incentives for "anti-social behavior."[2]

These "cultural triumphalists" (as one might call them in contrast to the "cultural declinists" Sullivan criticizes) have found their voice in such conservative organs as the *City Journal,* which has reported upon the considerable improvements in New York City in particular and in America as a whole. "Yessiree," Kay Hymowitz exults in an article entitled "It's Morning After in America," "family values are hot! Capitalism is cool! Seven-grain bread is so yesterday, and red meat is back!" Citing some of the now familiar statistics about crime, violence, abortions, and the like, she concludes that we are witnessing the emergence of "a vital, optimistic, family-centered, entrepreneurial, and yes, morally thoughtful, citizenry." This is a new kind of "bourgeois normality," she says, albeit one very different from the old. "The 1950s, this ain't."[3] But it is the 2000s, and a very good thing, too.

An earlier article in the same journal introduced still other evidence to explain why "We're Not Losing the Culture Wars Anymore." Brian Anderson cites three "seismic events": cable TV, the Internet, and book publishing, all of which provide conservative alternatives to what were once almost exclusively liberal domains. Cable TV, for example, gives us not only the Fox News channel but also Comedy Central's highest-rated program, the cartoon series *South Park*, featuring (this is Anderson's description) "four crudely animated and impossibly foul-mouthed fourth graders." The latter are Anderson's heroes, their "exuberant vulgarity" exposing the liberal pieties and PC mentality of the dominant culture. He quotes Andrew Sullivan who praised the show for being "the best antidote to PC culture we have," and who labeled its fans "South Park Republicans."[4] Anderson himself prefers "South Park Conservatives," the title of his recent book expanding upon his article.[5]

But it is more than the antiliberal, anti-PC thrust of the show that endears it to Anderson and qualifies it as "conservative." It is its vulgarity and raunchiness as well. He quotes one college student: "The label [South Park Republican] is really about rejecting the image of conservatives as uptight squares—crusty old men or nerdy kids in blue blazers. We might have long hair, smoke cigarettes, get drunk on weekends, have sex before marriage, watch R-rated movies, cuss like sailors—and also happen to be conservative, or at least libertarian."[6] One is reminded of the group of young, or not so young, conservative women some years ago who, in a similar effort to *épater les bourgeois*, flaunted their defiance of the conventional image of conservative womanhood by boasting that they could drink, cuss, smoke (cigars, not cigarettes), tell dirty jokes, and be as raunchy as the best of them.

To an old culture warrior like myself, South Park conservatism is an oxymoron, being not only antiliberal but anticonservative as well (and unfunny, to boot, its humor and pranks being more appropriate to fourth-grade louts than to sophomoric college students). It is disturbing, therefore, to find it being touted by serious conservatives. Conservatives, so astute about politics and economics, have always had difficulty coping with the culture. They were slow in coming to terms with the counterculture of the 1960s, in appreciating how much of a threat it was to the values and sensibilities, the social structures and institutions that had long been taken for granted. It was not until the counterculture had become the dominant culture that they began to take it seriously. And even then they were goaded to do so by religious groups who had taken its measure and had resisted it from the beginning, and who helped create, in effect, a counter-counterculture.

It is this counter-counterculture that is reflected in the statistics now cited by conservatives as evidence that they are winning the culture war. The statistics are encouraging and very welcome—but not, unhappily, altogether conclusive. If the divorce rate is stable (or very slightly falling), it is because fewer people are getting married, and the separation rate among couples living together without benefit of marriage is higher than the divorce rate among married couples. If the proportion of children in married-parent families rose by a single percent, that still leaves a third of the children with unmarried parents. If high school teenagers are drinking less and being less sexually active, college students are drinking more and being more active; binge-drinking and hooking up are major problems on many campuses. Young people may be less "alienated" from their parents than they used to be and more inclined to "believe in the values" of their parents.[7] But that is perhaps because their parents are more inclined to believe in the values of their children—not necessarily a sign of cultural maturity. (It would not be the first time that a generation of adults decided to surrender and call it victory.)

And so it goes for most of the other statistics. In any case, none of these indicators bring the family in particular, or the culture in general, back to the precounterculture situation. It has often been observed that in pre-counterculture 1965, when Senator Daniel Patrick Moynihan wrote his percipient report on the breakdown of the black family, the figure for black illegitimacy was lower than that for whites today and a fraction of that for blacks today. The conservative columnist David Brooks, who has been a staunch defender of the "culture war is dead" thesis, wrote one column presenting evidence that we are in the midst of a "moral revival," only to follow it with another piece three days later, based on other evidence, that concluded, "We are replacing marriage, one of our most successful institutions, with hooking up. This is a deep structural problem, and very worrying."[8]

There is another "structural problem" that does not lend itself to quantification but is no less troubling. Wolfe quotes my *One Nation, Two Cultures*, describing the situation as I saw it in 1999: "the collapse of ethical principles and habits, the loss of respect for authorities and institutions, the breakdown of the family, the decline of civility, the vulgarization of high culture, and the degradation of popular culture."[9] Vulgarization and degradation—one can hardly use those words today, any more than one can comfortably speak of indecency, incivility, or impropriety. They sound hopelessly prudish, old-fogyish, and—horrors!—judgmental; one is almost inclined to put quotation marks around them. Yet how can one take account of the coarsening (another no-no word) of the culture—the South Park culture—without such words. Moynihan once coined the phrase "defining deviancy down" to describe the situation: what was once stigmatized as deviant behavior is now tolerated; what was once regarded as abnormal has been normalized. Today, the very word "deviancy" is taboo.

Wolfe protests that the lives of "ordinary Americans" are not affected by the issues that have loomed so large in the culture war: the Schiavo case, abortion, gay marriage. But their lives are enormously affected, every day in every way, by the kind of culture symbolized by those South Park brats. That culture, the "popular culture"—the term is very apt—is most dramatically reflected in (and in part created by) television, movies, the Internet, and video games. In my book I quoted accounts of TV shows that were "pushing the envelope" with ever more egregious displays of violence, profanity, prurience, and promiscuity. "Like a child," the *New York Times* reported, "acting outrageously naughty to see how far he can push his parents, mainstream television this season [spring 1998] is flaunting the most vulgar and explicit sex, language, and behavior that it has ever sent into American homes."[10] One now rarely hears talk of "pushing the envelope" because the envelope has been pushed so far that reporters no longer think such language and behavior exceptionable or newsworthy.

"Where is the outrage?" Bill Bennett once asked, deploring the insufficient public reaction to President Clinton's sexual misconduct. When one event did elicit expressions of outrage—the breast-baring on the 2004 Super Bowl intermission (the "wardrobe malfunction," as it was delicately put)—journalists were taken aback by the reaction to what seemed to them to be a rather amusing episode. It was the outrage, more than the event itself, that was newsworthy. And it took something like a Superbowl intermission, that now-hallowed family occasion, to arouse dormant sensibilities and instincts. The public, almost as much as the press, has become inured to the escalating assaults upon traditional values.

Even a Bennett could not have envisaged the slew of reality shows that flaunt, even celebrate—and as "reality," not fiction—a degree of moral and esthetic nihilism (vulgarity, grossness, exhibitionism, and egregious materialism) that was once, if not quite unthinkable, certainly unviewable. And viewable now not only on cable channels that are unregulated but on the networks that presumably pass the test of regulators. The kind of casual, amiable promiscuity we got used to on *Friends* was replaced by the cold, calculating promiscuity of *Hooking Up*. (The titles themselves are suggestive, the one innocent and benign, the other unashamed and provocative.) Commenting on the last episode of the *Friends* series, the *New York Times* noted that the cast had "paired off in nearly every conceivable geometric combination over the years."[11] But at least that "pairing off" was among friends. *Hooking Up* (a documentary, not fiction) took place among strangers who meet on the Internet and coolly appraise each other; one participant cheerfully explains that she gives her dates twenty minutes to prove themselves worthy of her interest (that is, her bed).

Another pseudodocumentary, *The Aristocrats*, was hailed by the reviewer in the *New York Times* as "a work of painstaking and original scholarship, and, as such, one of the most original and rigorous pieces of criticism in any medium I have encountered in quite some time." This "essay film," the reviewer hastened to add, is "possibly the filthiest, vilest, most extravagantly obscene documentary ever made. . . . There is scarcely a minute of screen time that does not contain a reference to scatology, incest, bestiality, and practices for which no euphemisms or Latinate names have been invented."[12] The subject of the film is a single dirty joke, repeated 60 or 70 times (95 to 100 times, according to other counts)—a joke so dirty that it could not be printed in the *Times* or, so far as I know, any other respectable newspaper. My first thought on reading this review was that, of course, it was meant ironically. Not at all. The reviewer was quite serious in her admiration, as were the other reviewers cited in the ads for this "obscene, disgusting, vulgar and vile" film, the "funniest movie you'll ever see" (and a great commercial success).

As movies have been trumped by television and television by the Internet, so video games trump them all in being more accessible, more aggressive ("transgressive," in academese), and more addictive. The Internet prides itself on being interactive, but that is nothing compared with the interactive nature of video games—"virtual" (not merely passive) violence, sex, profanity, and wanton rage. One used to hear complaints about the time children spent watching TV. But that is nothing compared to the much more time-consuming and addictive nature of the Internet and video games, which can be indulged in private, without adult scrutiny. And not only by children but (as the evidence now suggests) by young and not so young adults, for whom these media have become so much the reality of their lives.[13]

Nor has the old medium, the written word, been laggard. A few years ago I wrote an article deploring what I took to be egregious examples of familial disloyalty and disrespect: a memoir by a well-known literary critic about his more distinguished wife, describing in excruciating detail her physical and mental degeneration as a result of Alzheimer's disease; another by a daughter about her prolonged (and voluntary) sexual relationship with her father (a minister); still another by a son about his father's (one of America's foremost intellectuals) putative (and entirely unproved) mental and moral debility.[14] Today, these demeaning and salacious memoirs are so common as to constitute an accepted literary genre. Not only celebrities but ordinary mothers and fathers, wives and lovers are fair game. "Mom died of Alzheimer yesterday," a piece in the *New York Times Magazine* opened.[15] "Yesterday"!—the son could not wait to rush into print. (Indeed, he must have prepared his piece, and it must have been accepted for publication, even printed, some time before her death.) Such revelations are by now so familiar that the reader is more inclined to be bored than shocked by them. And self-revelations as well. Confessions of marital infidelities or sexual perversities have at least some redeeming titillating quality. But what can be the appeal of an article by a respectable syndicated columnist in a respectable newspaper reporting, in graphic detail, on the frequency, texture, and quality of her bowel movements over the course of her lifetime?[16]

"Culture war" and "culture wars": the terms are used interchangeably. But perhaps the plural form is the more accurate. Conservatives (or, as James Hunter puts it, "traditionalists") may be winning the war over one sense of culture, that measured by the indices of crime, violence, illegitimacy, and the like. But they are losing the other war, the war over the popular culture—losing it by default, by sheer, willful inattention.

There are, to be sure, countervailing forces, people waging not war but a kind of passive resistance, opting out, so to speak, from the popular culture and founding a dissident culture of their own. Thus parents, displeased with the public school system (for moral as well as educational reasons), may choose, at considerable financial sacrifice, to send their children to private or religious schools, or (at even greater personal sacrifice) to teach them at home; more than a million children are now homeschooled. Professors, dissatisfied with the curriculum or mode of instruction in their colleges but knowing that it would be futile to try to transform or even reform them, may create (with the help of friendly foundations) oases in those institutions—centers, institutes, programs—that reflect their interests and values. And students, seeking something other than an aggressively secular education, may avail themselves of an ever expanding number of religious colleges. So, too, parents, despairing of the increasingly offensive fare on television and the Internet, no longer agitate for governmental regulation (or even self-regulation) of those media. Instead they act as their own regulators and censors. Some families adhere to what is called "TV abstinence," much as their youngsters commit themselves to "sexual abstinence."[17]

These groups represent something like a dissident culture—a valuable alternative to the dominant culture but hardly a victory over it. In this sense the culture wars are not over; they are only in abeyance. If conservatives are winning the body count, as measured by the statistics of crime, violence, abortion, and illegitimacy, they are losing the soul—the minds and hearts, the sensibilities and spirits of all too many people who are in thrall to the popular culture. That other war will have to be fought by other means and by other people. Not all has been won, by either side. But neither has all been lost.

Notes

1. Alan Wolfe, *One Nation, After All: What Middle Class Americans Really Think about God, Country, Family, Racism, Welfare, Immigration, Homosexuality, Work, the Right, the Left, and Each Other* (New York: Viking Penguin, 1998), p. 276.

2. Andrew Sullivan, "It's a Wonderful Life," *Times* (London), August 14, 2005.

3. Kay S. Hymowitz, "It's Morning After in America," *City Journal* 14 (Spring 2004): 56–57.

4. Brian C. Anderson, "We're Not Losing the Culture Wars Anymore," *City Journal* 13 (Autumn 2003): 15–21.

5. Brian C. Anderson, *South Park Conservatives: The Revolt against Liberal Media Bias* (Washington: Regnery, 2005).

6. Anderson, "Culture Wars," p. 22; *South Park Conservatives*, p. 99.

7. Hymowitz, "It's Morning After," p. 60.

8. David Brooks, "The Virtue of Virtues," *New York Times,* August 7, 2005, p. WK 12; "Sex and the Cities," *New York Times*, August 10, 2005, p. A27.

9. Gertrude Himmelfarb, *One Nation, Two Cultures* (New York: Knopf, 1999), p. 20.

10. Lawrie Mifflin, "TV Stretches Limits of Taste, to Little Outcry," *New York Times*, April 6, 1998, p. A1.

11. Tom Shales, "A Big Hug Goodbye to 'Friends' and Maybe to the Sitcom," *New York Times*, May 7, 2004, p. C1.

12. A. O. Scott, "A Filthy Theme and Variations," *New York Times*, July 29, 2005, p. B1. If I quote the *New York Times* so often, it is not only because I happen to read it but also because it is representative of respectable, mainstream journalistic opinion.

13. See Christine Rosen, "Playgrounds of the Self," *New Atlantis* (Summer 2005): 3–27.

14. Gertrude Himmelfarb, "A Man's Own Household His Enemies," *Commentary* 108, no. 1 (July 1999).

15. Steve Gettinger, "The Zen of Alzheimer's," *New York Times Magazine,* August 15, 1999, p. 68.

16. Jane E. Brody, "Looking Beyond Fiber to Stay 'Regular,'" *New York Times,* August 2, 2005.

17. These TV abstainers have been called "a band of internal exiles," recalling the "inner emigration" of dissidents in Nazi Germany who sought to retreat to a private haven uncontaminated by the regime. See Himmelfarb, *One Nation*, pp. 133–34.

COMMENT

FURTHER REFLECTIONS ON THE CULTURE WAR THESIS

MORRIS P. FIORINA

Academic scribblers soon learn that two things may happen when they set their arguments down on paper. First, no one may take notice, an unhappy but common outcome. Second, in the happier eventuality that fellow thinkers deem one's published thoughts sufficiently interesting to merit response, the original scribbler loses ownership of them. Published thoughts will be reinterpreted, amended, transported into different contexts, and otherwise transformed in ways not always anticipated by the originator who set them down.

James Davison Hunter is such a victim of his own success. He takes this occasion to object to some of the interpretations of his culture war thesis: "For my own part, the heart of the culture wars hypothesis was the contention that there had been a realignment in American public culture that had been and still is institutionalized chiefly through special interest organizations, denominations, political parties, foundations, competing media outlets, professional associations, and the elites whose ideals, interests, and actions give all of these organizations direction and leadership."

I have no quarrel with the preceding empirical proposition. To someone who grew up in the 1950s and 1960s such a realignment in public culture seems beyond dispute. But if Hunter believes that others have not interpreted his arguments in the manner that he had intended, it seems equally clear that he has not interpreted the arguments of others in the manner that they intended. For my own part, our critique of the culture war hypothesis was directed not at Hunter but at those in the media and in politics who claimed that the culture war not only extended down to the grass roots but was, in fact, the explanation or justification of why contemporary political campaigns do not appeal to the moderate middle and why elected representatives do not negotiate broadly acceptable compromises.[1] There is no straw man here; popular political commentary is replete with claims of widespread cultural conflict. For example, in explaining why President ("I am a uniter not a divider") Bush did not attempt to reach out beyond the Republican base, reelection strategist Matthew Dowd explained, "You've got 80 to 90 percent of the country that look at each other like they are on separate planets."[2] And yet, based on Hunter's own assertions, this statement would be far closer to the truth had Dowd put the range at 10 to 15 percent. In our work we took pains to show that while political elites may be engaged in a culture war, they are not reflecting popular preferences when they wield their cultural cudgels. Rather, as Philip Converse noted nearly a half century ago, the cognitive world of elites differs dramatically from that of normal Americans.[3]

However, while arguing that the culture war never had much of a mass base, I do not for a moment think that the culture war at the elite level is politically inconsequential. The authors whose work he cites—Brint; Smith; DiMaggio, Evans, and Bryson; Davis and Robinson; Rabkin; and Wolfe—can speak for themselves, but I think Hunter goes astray when he asserts that his critics arrived at "the authoritative conclusion that politically consequential normative conflict was simply nonexistent."[4] On the contrary, I wrote precisely because I was concerned about the political consequences of the elite culture war. Briefly, the immediate consequences are that voters are presented with polar alternatives—outlaw abortion or abortion on demand—when they would prefer something in between. (Splitting the difference is the American way.) Elites indulge in cultural battles—abortion, gay rights, gun control, the flag, the pledge, Terry Schiavo, stem cells—as if these were the most important problems facing the country, when polls consistently show that voters consider these minor issues. (Voters are concerned with such unexciting and TV-unfriendly issues as health care, jobs, education, and national security.) Culture warriors use their morally righteous stances to justify uncivil argument and behavior, the subjugation of evidence to faith and ideology, and refusal to compromise. (Normal Americans raise their children not to behave in these ways.)

The larger consequences of such a political order are more uncertain, of course, but the possibilities are by no means inconsequential. Such a political order fails to solve problems where simple ways to do so are clear (Social Security) and fails to address problems that—complex or not— must be addressed because crisis is close at hand (Medicare). Instead, such a political order wades into policy areas where public opinion would prefer that society be allowed to muddle through—Terry Schiavo, stem cells, medical marijuana.

Some believe that elite polarization eventually will percolate down and produce mass polarization. That would indeed be unfortunate, but I think the more likely prospect is that the elite culture war will produce further disengagement from politics on the part of normal Americans. In the 2004 presidential election, an increase in turnout to the 60 percent level produced considerable excitement, but this is about the turnout level that prevailed in 1960 when the culture war was some decades in the future. Despite the explosion of information sources, Americans are no better informed about politics—perhaps less informed—than they were a generation ago.[5] Despite the proliferation of participatory opportunities since the 1960s, Americans have not increased their participation correspondingly (except to write checks).[6] While such indicators of political disengagement have many causes—sociological, demographic, technological— I believe that at least some of the explanation is political. As Matthew Miller observes, "Alienation is the only intelligent response to a political culture that insults our intelligence."[7]

The main cause for optimism lies in my skepticism about another assumption made by Hunter, namely, the importance of elites. He writes:

> The development and articulation of the more elaborate systems of meaning and the vocabularies that make them coherent are more or less exclusively the realm of elites. . . . They are the ones who define and redefine the meaning of public symbols and provide the legitimating or delegitimating narratives of public figures or events. In all

of these ways and for all of these reasons, it is they and the strategically placed institutions they serve that come to frame the terms of public discussion.

Elites naturally like to believe in their own importance, but they tend to exaggerate it, and we often forget that numerous competing elites confuse the meanings and contest the narratives. My favorite example of the ineffectiveness of elites is the Lewinsky scandal when the great unwashed in the American public listened first to the national media and then to disbelieving Republican elites tell them that President Clinton was guilty of sexual harassment, abuse of his position, perjury, obstruction of justice and other transgressions, and who nevertheless answered firmly and consistently, "No, this is about sex, and I don't want to hear any more about it." On the other side, for more than a generation, Americans have listened to liberal elites justify various forms of racial, ethnic, and gender privilege with little effect on their private views. True, in a nod toward elites, Americans have learned to speak the politically correct language of diversity, but the words often are accompanied with a wink and a nudge.

Moreover, I suspect that the influence of elites is declining. We are no longer a minimally schooled nation with limited information sources. We have an educated population with more information sources than it can or wants to use. In addition, I think it true that more of today's elite consists of leaders without real followers. Rather than rise through the ranks of legitimate membership groups, many of the leaders of today's groups and organizations are self-selected political entrepreneurs. In Milton Rakove's wonderful phrase, they are the people "nobody sent."[8] They are less like the leaders of committed battalions and more like the nineteenth-century hucksters of patent medicines—and regarded similarly by skeptical Americans.

Finally, in defense of my fellow social scientists—at least political scientists—I do not agree that contemporary social science discounts conflict and celebrates consensus. Rather, empirical social scientists are doing their job—asking whether the facts on the ground support the grand theories that some attempt to erect on them. Where conflict exists, we will point it out and ponder its causes and consequences. Calling the culture war an intellectual "Potemkin village" does not mean that we will not identify conflict where it genuinely exists.

Turning now to Alan Wolfe's essay, he and I are on the same page regarding the culture war: it is (was?) an elite-driven phenomenon that never had a significant mass base and is now showing signs of exhaustion. But his emphasis on the importance of religion for American politics is welcome and contrasts with such a relative lack of emphasis in the political science literature. In the interest of self-preservation, I hasten to add that the American Political Science Association includes an organized section on religion and politics, established in 1983, with some 500 members who actively research and write on the subject, but I fear that the more traditional subfields of parties, elections, public opinion, and interest groups do not give such research the attention it merits. Even while writing about the campaign and lobbying activities of the religious right and the increasingly strong relationship between partisanship and religious commitment, there is a sense that the mainstream regards it as an aberration, perhaps because the mainstream is itself so secular.[9] The ratio of casual generalization about religion and politics to grounded research findings is higher than it should be in an academic discipline.

At any rate, Wolfe raises a number of issues that call for further research. For one thing, he suggests that the rise of the religious right was a reaction to the activities of religious left groups and sympathizers, an argument made by other sociologists in more specific contexts.[10] This argument brings up the general question of agenda formation—what issues are placed on the public agenda, by whom, when, and how? While there is some insightful work on the subject, we have little theory or even generalizations to fall back on.[11] How did we start down the road that led to a religious reaction, and what were the roles of elites and normal Americans in the process? In particular, the notion that liberal elites used nondemocratic institutions (courts and bureaucracies) to impose policies that would not have been imposed by elected officials has become standard fare in recent years. I believe the argument is correct, but it would be useful to have more systematic work on this subject.[12]

Wolfe notes an interesting paradox about contemporary America: the country has become more conservative politically while becoming more liberal culturally. This sounds correct, but I wonder if appearances deceive.

Our political system is majoritarian while the operation of our market economy is more akin to proportional representation of people, interest, and dollars. I doubt that a majority of states or congressional districts would vote to have the Michael Jackson trial televised all day, but the minority that would is sizable enough that commercial TV caters to their interest. More generally, I suspect that if unconstrained by the courts, a majority of states and congressional districts might well vote to ban soft-porn music videos and obscene CD lyrics, not to mention pornography. But there is sufficient demand from minorities that the free market meets it.[13] The rub, of course, is that popular culture has major external effects. Those who do not wish to be exposed to smut find it impossible to insulate themselves and their families from it, and the sense (probably accurate) that an offensive popular culture reflects minority interests and values only adds to the frustration.

Finally, it is important to emphasize once again—if only because the claim continues to be advanced in both the popular and academic literatures—that cultural issues have not eclipsed traditional economic issues. The divide between poorer and more affluent Americans in partisanship and voting has increased in recent decades, not decreased.[14] In 2004 the income gap between white Democratic and Republican voters was the third largest in the half century of presidential elections since 1952, and the largest when African Americans are included.[15] Tom Frank's *What's the Matter with Kansas?* is a terrific read—I was sorry when I came to the end—but its empirical assertions are almost completely wrong.[16] The Democrats will have to find other explanations for their current predicament.

Notes

1. Morris Fiorina, Samuel J. Abrams, and Jeremy C. Pope, *Culture War? The Myth of a Polarized America* (New York: Pearson Longman, 2005). We did not mention Hunter after page 2 of our book.

2. Quoted in Ron Brownstein, "Bush Falls to Pre-9/11 Approval Rating," *Los Angeles Times*, October 3, 2003, p. A1.

3. Philip Converse, "The Nature of Belief Systems in Mass Publics," in *Ideology and Discontent*, edited by David Apter (New York: Free Press, 1964).

4. Steven Brint, "What If They Gave a War . . . ?" *Contemporary Sociology* 21, no. 4 (1992): 438–40; Christian Smith and others, "The Myth of Culture Wars," *Culture: Newsletter of the Sociology of Culture, American Sociological Association* 11,

no. 1 (1996): 1, 7–10; Paul DiMaggio, John Evans, and Bethany Bryson, "Have Americans' Social Attitudes Become More Polarized?" *American Journal of Sociology* 102, no. 3 (1996): 690–755; Nancy Davis and Robert V. Robinson, "Are the Rumors of War Exaggerated? Religious Orthodoxy and Moral Progressivism in America," *American Journal of Sociology* 102, no. 3 (1996): 756–87; Nancy Davis and Robert V. Robinson, "Religious Orthodoxy in American Society: The Myth of a Monolithic Camp," *Journal for the Scientific Study of Religion* 35, no. 3 (1996): 229–45; Jeremy Rabkin, "The Culture War That Isn't," *Policy Review*, no. 96 (1999): 3–19; Alan Wolfe, *One Nation, After All: What Middle Class Americans Really Think about God, Country, Family, Racism, Welfare, Immigration, Homosexuality, Work, the Right, the Left, and Each Other* (New York: Viking Penguin, 1998), pp. 320–21.

5. Michael Delli Carpini and Scott Keeter, *What Americans Know about Politics and Why It Matters* (Yale University Press, 1996).

6. There was an increase in campaign participation in 2004, but it is the exception in a forty-year pattern, and its persistence remains to be seen.

7. Matthew Miller, "Is Persuasion Dead?" *New York Times*, June 4, 2005 (www. mattmilleronline.com/articles.php?id=145 [December 2005]).

8. Milton Rakove, *We Don't Want Nobody Nobody Sent* (Indiana University Press, 1979).

9. Or perhaps because political science is less historical than sociology and many of the past generation's researchers grew up during an era when religion played a relatively smaller role in politics than in much of American history.

10. For example, Kristin Luker in the context of the rise of the pro-life movement. See Kristin Luker, *Abortion and the Politics of Motherhood* (University of California Press, 1984).

11. See, for example, John Kingdon, *Agendas, Alternatives, and Public Policies* (Boston: Little, Brown, 1984). This book is widely and deservedly praised, but little by way of systematic literature has followed it.

12. Shep Melnick has done an admirable job of demonstrating such activities in the area of social welfare policy. It would be useful to have comparable studies in the area of moral issues other than abortion. R. Shep Melnick, *Between the Lines* (Brookings, 1994).

13. On the economics of news programming, see James Hamilton, *All the News That's Fit to Sell* (Princeton University Press, 2004).

14. Nolan McCarty, Keith Poole, and Howard Rosenthal, *Polarized America: The Dance of Ideology and Unequal Riches* (MIT Press, in press).

15. Morris Fiorina, Sam Abrams, and Jeremy Pope, *Culture War? The Myth of a Polarized America*, 2d ed. (New York: Pearson Longman, 2006), chap. 7.

16. Thomas Frank, *What's the Matter with Kansas? How Conservatives Won the Heart of America* (New York: Henry Holt, 2004). For further discussion, see Larry Bartels, "What's the Matter with *What's the Matter with Kansas?*" *Quarterly Journal of Political Science*, in press.

A RESPONSE FROM
JAMES DAVISON HUNTER

ONE WAY TO gain clarity in the debate over the culture war is to make a distinction between "the politics of culture" and "the culture of politics." On the face of it, these phrases may seem to refer to the same thing. They each contain the same words, after all; confusion is understandable. But there is an important difference implied by the two statements, a difference that goes to the heart of this debate.

The Politics of Culture and the Culture of Politics

The "politics of culture" refers to the push and pull of the mechanisms of power over cultural issues. Within democratic regimes, of course, this would include the mobilization of parties (for example, the leading politicians, their respective organizations, the financial resources, and the rank-and-file support), the formation of coalitions among interest groups, and the manipulation of public rhetoric on matters reflecting the symbols or ideals at the heart of a "cultural" issue. Thus, for instance, the fight over abortion is a fight of social movements and political parties over the policies surrounding this symbolically freighted and highly divisive issue. This is what some refer to as postmaterialist or "expressive politics."

In contradistinction is the "the culture of politics," by which I mean the symbolic environment within which political institutions are embedded and political action occurs. This symbolic environment is constituted by

the basic frameworks of meaning that make particular political arrange-
ments understandable or incomprehensible, desirable or reprehensible.
These basic frameworks of implicit meaning constitute a culture's "deep
structure." It is similar in some ways to what Charles Taylor has called
"social imaginaries" or what Pierre Bourdieu has called *habitus*, but especially as it refers to the ontology of the social order—its implicit structure
of authority, anthropology, collective narrative, and the like.[1] Without
these deep structures, certain political institutions and practices simply
do not make any sense. Politics may protect a particular social order but
does not shape it, lead it, or guide it. As the political philosopher Michael
Oakeshott once put it, "A political system presupposes a civilization; it has
a function to perform in regard to that civilization, but it is a function
mainly of protection and to a minor degree of merely mechanical interpretation and expression." Thus "political activity may have given us
Magna Carta and the Bill of Rights, but it did not give us the contents of
these documents, which came from a stratum of social thought far too
deep to be influenced by the actions of politicians."[2] The same can be said
for the Declaration of Independence, the Treaty of Versailles, the UN
Charter for Human Rights, and the Kyoto Accord; political activity may
have produced these documents, but it did not provide their substance.
These, too, came from a framework of sensibility and understanding more
implicit than the explicit deliberations and decisions of the architects of
these documents.

In the former case, culture is implicated at every level. That said, the
"politics of culture" is mainly about politics. Likewise, in the latter case,
power and politics are also implicated at every level. Yet here, too, the
"culture of politics" is primarily about the culture.

How do these distinctions bear on the debate over the existence or
nonexistence of the culture war? The critics of the culture wars hypothesis all operate within the "politics of culture" perspective. To give exclusive
attention to elections and campaigns, administrations, the voting behavior among Democrats and Republicans, and party ideology, and to talk
about "political miscalculations" and the political sidelining of those who
misguidedly continue to fight this conflict all makes politics the frame of
reference in their argument. Advocates of the culture wars hypothesis,

like me, align with the "culture of politics" approach. In this case, the focus is on *normative* conflict. The political consequences of this conflict are significant, of course, but that is not the primary concern. The focus, rather, is on the symbolic dimensions of the conflict, the nature and institutional structures and dynamics of the discourse, the competing sources of authority that animate the conflict, and so on.

In this light, it is hardly surprising that advocates and critics of the culture wars hypothesis come to different conclusions. It is not just that they are approaching matters differently. They are actually analyzing different things. The debate, such as it is, comprises different analytical strategies that do not quite address the same data.

A Vital Center?

Leaving aside the question of how or whether it bears on the culture war, it goes without saying that the "politics of culture" approach is an important analytical strategy for understanding the dynamics of contemporary American democracy. At this level I find myself very much in agreement with many of the arguments of Alan Wolfe and Morris Fiorina here and elsewhere. While the moral questions that animate issues such as abortion, gay rights, assisted suicide, and the like are enduring, the specific policy questions surrounding them will come and go and as such will be used to political advantage when it seems appropriate to do so.

Understood in this way, cultural politics, in fact, has been the domain of the Republicans. Over the last two and a half decades, they have been the party that has most self-consciously (and shamefully, at times) manipulated public sentiment on these issues for their political gain. It is they, too, who have been most effective at mobilizing the grass roots. By and large, their political calculus has worked in their favor from issue to issue. But it has not worked all of the time. For example, it was extremely well honed in their use of traditional marriage amendments in the 2004 election. Republicans understood the moral sensibilities of their conservative constituencies and were able to manipulate them very effectively into political mobilization. It was not just the traditionalism that they understood but also the level of fear and resentment these conservatives felt toward the moral libertarianism of the Democratic left. Whatever else they accomplished, the Republicans got out the vote in districts and regions where voters could just as well have stayed home—most important, in Ohio. By contrast, Republican cultural politics was utterly ill conceived in the Terry Schiavo case. Here, party operatives completely misread the contradictory attitudes of their constituencies and the public as a whole. Overall, though, political conservatives have used these issues far more effectively than political liberals, which helps account for so much of the former's dominance in American politics since the 1980s.

Operating out of the "politics of culture" perspective, one clearly sees the distinction between elites and masses. The politics of culture really is the province of political operatives, and the fissures among them are in their interest to cultivate. But what about the electorate? Is the electorate so divided? From this vantage point (the exception noted in the earlier essay notwithstanding), Wolfe, Fiorina, and others are partly right when they observe that conflict is *not* reflected so deeply in public sentiment. In making this observation, some have implied or stated outright that this means that there is a corresponding consensus in American public attitudes, that an underlying unity is the real story of America today, that America is "one nation after all."

Here, though, one should be cautious. As my colleague Joseph Davis has put it, to say that conflict is not the main story is not the same thing as arguing that citizens are becoming more civic minded, that political participation is increasing, or that concern for the most vulnerable members of our society is growing.[3] The evidence would suggest otherwise. Indeed, if there is a center in American politics today, it is certainly not "the vital center" that Arthur Schlesinger Jr. described at midcentury.[4] What "center" exists seems to be mostly passive and contentless, a function of a massive disaffection of the public with politics as usual. E. J. Dionne Jr.'s argument in *Why Americans Hate Politics* is right, then.[5] This center is not clear and purposeful in its vision for the future or coherent in its political ideals. This is not to say that there are no civic-minded people or organizations that aspire to such vitality on behalf of the common good. Rather, it is only to say that such vitality is not represented by any political party or by any particular mass social movement.

The Priority of Culture over Politics

We live in a time when everything seems to be either monetized or politicized. In the case of political scandal, it is both. (There is money to be made in political schadenfreude!) Politicization means that politics defines the primary frame of action and significance for social life or parts of it. With the ever-proliferating special interest organizations, lobbying and litigation is, of course, their daily fare. But tendencies toward politicization reach far beyond this realm into nearly every part of civil society as well. In journalism (even on education, science, art, family, and so on), reporting is all too often reduced to the narrative of winners and losers in the struggle for power. Professional organizations lend their legitimacy to one side of the controversy or the other, even when there is no clear and intrinsic relationship between expertise and advocacy. In religious organizations ideology is often elevated over theology to such an extent that the public witness of faith in our day has become a partisan and political witness. This is no less true in academia, where scholarly contribution is often classified politically before it is engaged intellectually. Throughout civil society, partisan, political, and legal objectives define the identity of groups and the priorities of their public agenda. In a culture that has been so thoroughly politicized, it is hardly surprising that a perspective oriented to the "politics of culture" is given precedence over one oriented to the "culture of politics."

I have a different take on this. In my view politicization may be the most visible aspect of the present normative conflict, but that also makes it the most ephemeral and, therefore, the least important part of the story. The reason is that culture nearly always leads politics, not the other way around. Thus, for example, a sea change in the acceptance of homosexuality and gay rights by educated professionals and the resymbolization of gay life in art and media long preceded its acceptance in law and public policy. Laws protecting the rights of women followed popular acceptance, especially within the upper middle classes. And so on. Culture frames concerns, legitimates claims, and articulates arguments that are then ratified by law and policy. As I say, culture tends to lead and politics tends to follow.

Politics will and must change almost on a daily basis. The movements of culture, however, are far slower. Attention given to the observable and behavioral aspects of conflict tends to make one inattentive to what is occurring in the deep structures of cultural change in our moment in history, to the ways it relates to epochal shifts we speak of when we talk of late modernity. Not least among these are the subtle but profound shifts in the nature and dynamics of authority.

If this is true, then, America's move to the right politically and to the left culturally is highly portentous. It means that the religious right is wrong to be confident and that progressives are wrong to fret; cultural conservatives will likely lose this struggle for power. They have sought political solutions as a way of addressing issues that are deeply cultural—and not just issues, but taste, manners, morality, and authority. Cultural conservatives bet on politics as the means to respond to the changes in the world, but that politics can only be a losing strategy. What political solution is there to the absence of decency? To the spread of vulgarity? To the lack of civility and the want of compassion? The answer, of course, is none—there are no political solutions to these concerns, and the headlong pursuit of them by conservatives will lead, inevitably, to failure.

Politics is neither the best nor the exclusive form of public activity. Yet we give far too much credence to it. Our expectations for what it can accomplish are too high. The Christian right is wrong on this no less than the secular left. But so are all who look to politics for solutions. In "Why the Culture War Is the Wrong War," for example, E. J. Dionne Jr. wrote that "the culture war exploits our discontents. The task of politics is to heal them."[6] Even at its best, politics represents a simplification and vulgarization of sensibilities found in culture. Politics has its place, and that place is critically important, of course. Politics can provide a platform for dissent, rituals of consensus, and the procedures for pursuing social justice and public order. But to ask politics to do anything more than solve administrative problems, much less "heal" a divided social order, may be asking too much. Though it is dominant in our society, it is of secondary importance. Liberal democracy is not just a political structure; it is first and foremost a political culture: a myth, a set of ideals, a discourse, and the habits of mind, belief, and relationship that sustain it. Until liberal democracy is renewed at the level of its cultural substructure, politics, and political expedience, may only further denigrate public life, even if it proceeds in the name of lofty and admirable political ideals.

Notes

1. Charles Taylor, *Modern Social Imaginaries* (Duke University Press, 2004); and Pierre Bourdieu, *Outline of a Theory of Practice* (Cambridge University Press, 1977).

2. Michael Oakeshott, *Religion, Politics, and the Moral Life*, edited by Timothy Fuller (Yale University Press, 1993), p. 93.

3. Joseph Davis, review of *The Fractious Nation*, edited by Jonathan Rieder, *Contemporary Sociology* 33 (2004): 703–04.

4. Arthur Schlesinger Jr., *The Vital Center* (Boston: Houghton-Mifflin, 1949).

5. E. J. Dionne Jr., *Why Americans Hate Politics* (New York: Simon and Schuster, 1991).

6. E. J. Dionne Jr., "Why the Culture War Is the Wrong War," *Atlantic Monthly*, January–February 2006 p. 135.

A RESPONSE FROM
ALAN WOLFE

MORRIS FIORINA EXPRESSES my own thoughts with respect to one point raised by James Davison Hunter. Of those who have questioned the extent of the American culture war, Hunter writes, "These critics argued, in effect, that nothing of particular consequence was occurring [in American politics] at all." Nowhere, Fiorina replies, has he made a claim along those lines. Nor have I. Much has happened of great consequence in American politics since the 1970s: politics has become more partisan; candidates rely more on focus groups; issues that focus on moral and cultural matters, at least for a time, displaced those dealing with economics and foreign policy; and both parties have relied to a much greater extent than before on those who constitute their ideological base. What has not happened, or so I argue along with Fiorina and other critics of the culture war hypothesis, is that the ideological extremism among policy elites has been matched by a corresponding ideological extremism among the majority of ordinary Americans.

I have tried to be clear, both in my book and in the essay I have written for this volume, that something called a "culture war" exists among the political leadership class in this country. I also agree with Hunter that local culture wars have been fought in school districts and near city halls around the country. It does no good, therefore, to say, as Gertrude Himmelfarb does, that I contradict my own insistence that no culture war exists by claiming that the culture war is on its last legs. On the contrary, I am saying that even though over the past few decades our elites have been engaged in a culture war, now, in the wake of events like the Schiavo fiasco, not even they find much value in insisting on our irreconcilable cultural differences.

Himmelfarb describes herself as an "old culture warrior" and goes on to express her feeling that a society that welcomes the vulgar trash called American popular entertainment is a society in serious decline. May I try to persuade her that even people who would never describe themselves as culture warriors—I am here talking about myself—share her disgust with much of American popular culture? When Bill Bennett, Dolores Tucker, and Joe Lieberman sent out a call to denounce this stuff, I signed it, even though I am generally averse to signing public petitions. Surely Himmelfarb must realize that breast-bearing Super Bowl halftimes have more to do with market share and earnings reports than with left-wing activists trying to impose their unpopular views on the majority. The problem with American popular culture is that it is, well, popular. This explains why Republicans, for all their talk of moral values, are willing to accept political contributions from cable television companies that feature pornography. Once upon a time, Coors beer fought for right-wing causes. Now it advertises using images of wild parties and near-naked females. I only wish we had a culture war over popular culture; then at least one side would stand up for classical music and serious art. The fact that there is no side in opposition to popular culture suggests that, on this issue, we have no war at all, cultural or otherwise.

And this brings to me back to James Hunter and the many disagreements I have with his way of talking about these issues. Hunter suggests three areas of difference between himself and his critics: methodology, empirical reality, and theoretical assumptions. Each of them deserves a response.

In his essay for this volume, Hunter acknowledges his debt to "the structural turn in cultural analysis." Culture, from this point of view, does not engage itself so much with "the norms and values residing in people's heads and hearts" but concentrates on "systems of symbols and other cultural artifacts, the institutions that produce and promulgate those symbols, discourses that articulate and legitimate particular interests, and competing fields where culture is contested." This cultural turn, he believes, enables scholars of modern societies to dig deeper than they do when they merely register opinion through polls and surveys. Scholars should rely on the "rigorous conceptualization" of culture first developed by Emile Durkheim and elaborated by contemporary writers such as Niklas Luhmann and Mary Douglas.

For Hunter, in other words, writers such as Fiorina and myself took the easy way out by concentrating on culture in its most superficial forms; had we been more serious, we would have dealt with "the structures of culture that produce and distribute symbols, ideas, arguments, and ideologies." To this charge Fiorina responds by saying that he uses a popular conception of culture because that is the one favored by so many media commentators on American politics; his concern is with them and not with academic theorists. My response is somewhat different. I believe that the concept of culture that Hunter finds so rigorous and compelling is actually problematic for both scholarship and citizenship.

One of the unfortunate consequences of neo-Durkheimian conceptions of culture is that they reify structures at the expense of the individuals who live within them. To give readers a flavor of what this means, one need only cite the title of a book by Mary Douglas: *How Institutions Think*.[1] Douglas's aim is admirable: she wants us to understand how institutions develop patterns of behavior that over time take on a life of their own. Anyone who has ever tried to understand the FBI will appreciate what Douglas explores. Yet institutions do not think; only the people who have shaped them over time do. Structural theories invariably downplay the extent to which institutions change because they fail to account for the ways in which new cohorts of people, by behaving and thinking differently than those who came before them, transform the institutional world around them.

What is true of institutions is also true of culture. In Hunter's account institutions of cultural production become invested in the idea of culture war in order to mobilize resources or to sustain their identity. Over time, the conflicts they promote become "a reality *sui generis*, a reality much larger—indeed, autonomous from—the sum total of individuals and organizations that give expression to the conflict." But if Hunter is right, then how do we explain that issues that were once central to the culture war—say, issues involving race, which became the first real wedge issues in contemporary American politics—lose their saliency over time while others that did not even exist twenty years ago—for example, stem cell research—become issues in political campaigns? These kinds of events occur precisely because the culture war is not autonomous from the people who fight it. It has no reality of its own; whatever reality it has is in fact tenuous and temporary. That is why political leaders cannot take the culture war for granted; if it had the autonomy of which Hunter speaks, politicians would always appeal to it. But, as I insisted in my contribution to this volume, Republicans both arouse moral concerns with talk of abortion and gay rights and then dampen them by never following through on their rhetoric, as if they understand that the culture war is anything but a fixed reality.

There are more than academic issues involved in the attempt to treat culture as part of a structure impervious to human action. It is right and proper to focus on survey data and opinion polling when dealing with the culture war hypothesis because the views of ordinary people count in a democracy. This is something that conservatives frequently point out; it is wrong, they say, for undemocratic branches of government such as the Supreme Court to preempt the democratic political process on an issue such as abortion. Unlike many on the left, I agree with conservatives on this point. For the same reason, however, I am distrustful of those who argue that structures put a culture war in place even if ordinary people do not want one to exist; in a democracy, after all, people themselves should not only be allowed to express their preferences on abortion, they should also have a say on the question of whether they will allow an issue such as abortion to divide them. To claim that a culture war exists over and above the choices and desires of real people is to downplay free will, one reason why structural theories have so long been identified with Marxists and postmodernist literary theorists. We should be wary of such structural approaches, not only because they do a bad job explaining how structures change but because they come accompanied by conceptions of human nature that do not assign sufficient creativity to human ingenuity. When structures have autonomy, people do not.

Hunter next turns to empirical questions, and here, it turns out, there is not much disagreement between him and his critics. He says, quite rightly, that his own research has demonstrated the extent to which the middle portion of American opinion does not correspond with more extreme views on either side. In some of his other empirical work, more-over, Hunter uncovers aspects of American society very similar to those of his critics. To cite only one example, the pervasive nonjudgmentalism I found in American opinion corresponds with Hunter's finding, in *The Death of Character*, of how Americans, including American elites, have lost touch with conceptions of individual virtue.[2] There is a broad empirical consensus among social scientists about the extent to which ordinary Americans are attracted to ideological extremes: most of Americans—certainly a majority—are not.

Majorities, by definition, do not include everyone, and it is therefore perfectly proper to examine the attitudes of those who do locate themselves at either extreme. Here, though, Hunter and I do have a strong disagreement. He believes that one extreme is composed of traditionalists, people who, in his view, seek "deliberate continuity with the ordering principles inherited from the past." In the other camp, he writes, are "progressivists," people who idealize "experimentation and thus adaptation and innovation with the changing circumstances of our time." I have no doubt that one can find traditional and progressive people in America. I have great doubt that they line up against each other in the culture war.

Just about everyone who writes about the culture war says that the traditionalists are religious believers who view the increasing secularization of America with dismay. But as I insist in both *The Transformation of American Religion* and my essay in this book, such a description does not apply to evangelicals.[3] To be born again is to reject the lessons of one's past and to embrace a new identity. It is to value authenticity of belief over beliefs that have long creedal histories behind them. It is no wonder that so many Republican voters do not live in traditional families; the divorce rate in Oklahoma is three times what it is in Massachusetts. These conservative voters are seekers; they are searching for truths far more than they are defending truth. They switch their faiths for the same reason that they remarry or relocate. They are among the most mobile, the most experimental, of all Americans.

Liberals, by contrast, as the low rates of divorce in Massachusetts suggest, are often traditionalists at heart. They are the ones who write—and presumably buy—all the books about the Founding Fathers; without them and their support for public television, America would barely have a history.

They are the ones left behind in the cold states as their more conservative neighbors move to Scottsdale or Alpharetta. Their churches still have organs, and their schools prepare students for colleges founded in the eighteenth century. The academics among them have tenure, and no one in America is more conservative than a leftist faculty member with job security. I verge on caricature here, but I hope my point has been made. Traditionalism and innovation are concepts that have more to do with personality types than with religious and political beliefs. Or, to put the matter another way, a person can be found in the extreme right-wing or left-wing end of the political spectrum because their ideas are right wing or left wing. It is not their approach to modernity that defines them. It is their views on specific issues and candidates.

One of Hunter's most valuable contributions to the debate over the culture war is his belief that traditionalists in different religions have more in common with each other than they do with liberals within their own religion. On this point, Hunter's claims have been accurate. Conservative Protestants, Catholics, and Jews have congregated around the Republican Party, while liberal Protestants, Catholics, and Jews have gone the other way. We used to fight between religions, as our awful history of anti-Catholicism and anti-Semitism shows. We now fight within them; Episcopalians disagree with each other over homosexuality more than they do with Catholics over the liturgy. This is a major, and most likely positive, change; it insulates us against the religious wars that have plagued not only our own history but that of Europe as well.

But if Hunter was right on this point in the past, I am not sure he will be right in the future. Think, for a moment, of the implications that follow from this religious realignment. If conservative Protestants, Catholics, and Jews line up on the same side, they are essentially claiming that their politics matter to them more than their faith; whatever differences over infant baptism or the literal truth of Scripture that divided them in the past, now it is only positions on abortion or gay marriage that matter. But why then, if politics matters so much, have religion at all? And how can conservative religious believers claim to be traditionalists if they are so quick to overthrow a long-standing tradition, at least in evangelical Protestantism, of separating matters of politics from matters of faith? If Hunter is right that there is a new realignment among religions, he is acknowledging that religion itself is less meaningful. If he is wrong, then the agreement between conservatives of all faiths on the one side and liberals of all faiths on the other will prove temporary.

The latter possibility is the more likely one because the conservative political alliance among faiths is already under considerable strain. Without confronting explicitly political conservative Protestants by name, evangelicals such as Rick Warren and the leaders of the National Association of Evangelicals are distancing themselves from the direct involvement in conservative politics promoted by Baptist leaders such as Richard Land or media figures such as Jerry Falwell. Whether the issues are the environment or AIDS in Africa, an increasing number of prominent evangelical Protestants are trying to focus on social issues more directly linked to their religious mission than on political issues that would align them with one political party. In this way they are in fact more "traditionalist" than their explicitly conservative brethren because they are engaged in reclaiming the separation between faith and politics that once featured so prominently in evangelical religions. The interesting question for American politics is whether they will have support in the pews for their efforts to distance themselves from the American culture war. My guess—and it is at this point only a guess—is that they sense a growing discomfort in the megachurches with the attempt by Falwell, James Dobson, and others to link Protestantism to the fortunes of the Republican Party.

Similar tensions can be found among the other faiths that have contributed to the realignment among religions about which Hunter has written. A few Catholic bishops distanced themselves from John Kerry's pro-choice views in 2004 without criticizing similar views among Republican Catholics such as Rudy Giuliani, George Pataki, and Arnold Schwarzenegger. But this blatant partisanship had little effect on most American Catholics, who respectfully disagree with the Church's teachings on most issues involving sexual reproduction and who, in any case, remain deeply skeptical of the leadership of their church in the wake of its sexual abuse crisis. Catholics are, in general, more likely to vote Republican these days than they were a generation or two ago, but this has more to do with their rising socioeconomic status than with culture war issues. And there is considerable reason to doubt that Catholics, unlike more schismatic Protestants, ever allowed their political differences to trump their religious ones; whether conservative or liberal, most American Catholics share a communal outlook on the world distinct from the more individualistic ethic of Protestantism.

Nor, finally, do American Jews line up along political lines. Some extremely conservative Jews have formed an alliance with evangelicals over the support the latter have given to Israel. But even in the face of the electoral victory of Hamas, there are tensions within Israel between the hard-right politicians whom evangelicals tend to support and those, such as Ariel Sharon, who looked for possible avenues of negotiation with the Palestinians. Finally, Americans Jews from all denominations worry that the Christian right aims to Christianize the United States, not a prospect that any Jew of any political persuasion can easily accept. In other words, since Hunter published *Culture Wars*, there has been little progress toward a further realignment among religions and some movement in the opposite direction.[4]

Hunter's final point is a theoretical one. If we want to understand society, are we better off assuming the existence of consensus and looking for conflict, or assuming conflict and searching for consensus? Hunter argues for the latter. His reasons have much to do with the concept of culture he finds so rigorous. "Where there is culture, there is struggle"—the words belong to Philip Rieff, but the sentiments are those of Hunter.[5] Cultures establish themselves through duality: purity versus danger, good against evil, us and them. Culture is essential to maintaining the identity of a group, and groups survive by distinguishing themselves from others. From such a perspective, the term culture war is redundant; wherever there is culture, there is war. Culture, Hunter writes, is "by its very nature, contested—always and everywhere, even when it appears most homogeneous."

I find this way of theorizing about culture problematic for the same reason I reject Hunter's structuralism: if one accepts the way Hunter defines culture, there is nothing much left to investigate. Since we have a culture war automatically by having culture, the only question worth pursuing is whether our cultural war is serious or deadly serious. Why organize conferences and publish books debating the question of whether a culture war exists? One side in that debate—my side, as it happens—is ruled out of order before the debate even begins.

Hunter is surprised that critics of the culture war hypothesis adhere to what he believes to be a thoroughly obsolete method of social science theorizing. In his view people such as me subscribe to a "social science [that] looks very much like the establishment and consensus-oriented structural functionalism of the mid-twentieth century." For veterans of the 1960s, these are fighting words. I spent decades dissenting from the consensus-driven social theories of sociologists such as Talcott Parsons; now I stand accused of being sympathetic to them.

So let me plead guilty as charged. Scholars who emphasized the importance of consensus in the 1950s were reacting to decades of vehement ideological conflict in Europe; compared to communist and fascist dictatorships, America, and its moderate centrism, seemed the best possible alternative. To be sure, there did exist American versions of ideological politics: some members of the consensus school had been active in the Marxist politics of the 1930s and were reacting against their former radicalism. Others noted, even if they did not attach all that much significance to the fact, the emergence of a radical right, whether among the followers of Senator McCarthy or in extremist organizations such as the John Birch Society. They had little doubt, however, that liberalism would triumph over extremism. The genius of American politics, as Daniel Boorstin put it, lay in its nonideological pragmatism.[6]

In the decades since consensus-oriented scholars wrote, extremist politics has come to our shores. Fortunately, we have nothing resembling the totalitarian movements of the 1930s and 1940s. But the extreme right movements that seemed so small in the years right after World War II now occupy prominent places in one of America's two major parties. Extremist voices, at times advocating violence, dominate our airwaves. Bitter partisanship characterizes our politics in ways not seen since the nineteenth century. Each party appeals to its activist base. No party or candidate has emerged, at least not at this writing, to mobilize the moderate center. When events as tragic as September 11 divide us rather than unite us, we are in deep political trouble.

Under such conditions, I believe that the proper response, on both scholarly and normative grounds, is to start an investigation into American society by assuming a certain degree of consensus before looking for conflict. The empirical justification is that the consensus is there and is more representative of American opinion than the extremes. Given that Hunter agrees on empirical grounds that the majority of Americans are in the center, I fail to understand why he should not begin where they are.

The normative ground for a consensus-first approach is that liberal societies work best when they defuse ideological conflict in favor of the common good and, when that is not possible, in favor of neutrality between different conceptions of the common good. James Davison Hunter is right to assert that when we argue about the culture wars, we are arguing about the future of liberalism. If we believe that liberalism offers what Hunter calls "a framework for toleration, freedom, and justice," we need to be reminded of everything we Americans hold in common even as we acknowledge the issues that divide us. That goal is not achieved by insisting that we must always be divided because culture is divisive. On the contrary, we must recognize that we would not be a society in the first place unless we treasured the same values.

Of all my disagreements with Hunter, this is the most serious. He argues that because liberalism protects diversity, we must avoid denying the deep differences among us. I insist that our differences are political rather than cultural or religious; we disagree over abortion or gay marriage because some of us are conservatives and others are liberals, not because some of us are religious and others secular. Political differences will and should always exist in a democracy; we have political institutions—parties, elections, surveys—to register those differences and deal with their consequences. Cultural and religious differences are more difficult to negotiate, but the United States has done a pretty good job on that score as well, absorbing large numbers of immigrants and insisting on a common creed to moderate our cultural diversity. Despite its turn to the right in recent years, America remains, much as Louis Hartz insisted more than half a century ago, committed to the political philosophy of John Locke.[7] We are united by our liberal commitment to individualism.

It is a miracle for any society to achieve consensus; look at the difficulties facing the Iraqis because they cannot. It is especially difficult for a society as large and complex as our own to have developed widespread commitments to a democratic way of life. The culture war being waged by so many of our leaders—the same one increasingly viewed by ordinary people as being as divisive as it is ugly—fails to meet the broadly liberal standards of tolerance and pluralism that have guided this country for so long. Our best hope to protect and extend the liberal spirit of tolerance and fair play that has made us a great nation is to build on the consensus among ordinary people as a counter to the extremism that characterizes so much of our current political elite. If I am going to begin anywhere in understanding my country, I want to begin not when it is acting at its worst but when it is living up to its best.

Notes

1. Mary Douglas, *How Institutions Think* (Syracuse University Press, 1986).

2. James Davison Hunter, *The Death of Character: Moral Education in an Age without Good or Evil* (New York: Basic Books, 2000).

3. Alan Wolfe, *The Transformation of American Religion: How We Actually Live Our Faith* (New York: Free Press, 2003).

4. James Davison Hunter, *Culture Wars: The Struggle to Define America* (New York: Basic Books, 1991).

5. See Hunter's essay in this volume, p. 34.

6. Daniel Boorstin, *The Genius of American Politics* (University of Chicago Press, 1953).

7. Louis Hartz, *The Liberal Tradition in America: An Interpretation of American Political Thought Since the Revolution* (New York: Harcourt, Brace, and World, 1955).

CONTRIBUTORS

MICHAEL CROMARTIE is vice president at the Ethics and Public Policy Center, where he directs both the Evangelicals in Civic Life and Religion and Media programs. He is a senior adviser to the Pew Forum on Religion and Public Life; a senior fellow with the Trinity Forum; and an advisory editor of *Christianity Today*. He is the editor of fourteen books, including, most recently, *Religion, Culture, and International Conflict* (2005) and *Religion and Politics in America* (2005). He was appointed by President George W. Bush to the U.S. Commission on International Religious Freedom and has served as chair and vice-chair of the commission.

E.J. DIONNE JR. is a senior fellow in Governance Studies at the Brookings Institution and University Professor in the Foundations of Democracy and Culture at Georgetown University. He is also a syndicated columnist with the *Washington Post* and a senior adviser to the Pew Forum on Religion & Public Life. He is the author of *Why Americans Hate Politics* (2nd ed., 2004), *Stand Up Fight Back* (2004), and *They Only Look Dead* (1996). He is also the editor or coeditor of several Brookings volumes including *Sacred Places, Civic Purposes* (2001), *What's God Got to Do with the American Experiment?* (2000), and *Community Works: The Revival of Civil Society in America* (1998).

MORRIS P. FIORINA is a senior fellow at the Hoover Institution and the Wendt Family Professor of Political Science at Stanford University. He is the coauthor of *Culture War: The Myth of a Polarized America*

(2nd ed., 2005), with Samuel J. Abrams and Jeremy C. Pope. Earlier he published numerous articles and books including *Divided Government* (2nd ed., 1996), *Congress—Keystone of the Washington Establishment* (1989), and *Home Style and Washington Work* (1989), coedited with David Rohde. *The Personal Vote: Constituency Service and Electoral Independence* (1987), coauthored with Bruce Cain and John Ferejohn, won the 1988 Richard F. Fenno Prize. He is also coeditor of *Continuity and Change in House Elections.*

GERTRUDE HIMMELFARB is professor emeritus of the Graduate School of the City University of New York. She is a member of the Council of Scholars of the Library of Congress and a fellow of the British Academy and of the American Academy of Arts and Sciences. Her most recent books are *The Moral Imagination* (2006) and *The Roads to Modernity* (2004). Among her other books are *One Nation, Two Cultures* (2001); *The De-Moralization of Society* (1995); *On Looking into the Abyss* (1994); *Poverty and Compassion* (1991); and intellectual biographies of Darwin, Acton, and Mill.

JAMES DAVISON HUNTER is the LaBrosse-Levinson Professor of Religion, Culture and Social Theory at the University of Virginia and the director of the Institute for Advanced Studies in Culture. He is the author of *The Death of Character: Moral Education in an Age without Good or Evil* (2000), *Culture Wars: The Struggle to Define America* (1991), *Before the Shooting Begins: Searching for Democracy in America's Culture War* (1994), *Evangelicalism: The Coming Generation* (1987), and *American Evangelicalism: Conservative Religion and the Quandary of Modernity* (1983). In 2005 he was awarded the Richard M. Weaver Prize for Scholarly Letters.

ALAN WOLFE is professor of political science and director of the Boisi Center for Religion and American Public Life at Boston College. His most recent books include *Does American Democracy Still Work?* (2006), *Return to Greatness: How America Lost Its Sense of Purpose and What It Needs to Do to Recover It* (2005), *The Transformation of American Religion: How We Actually Practice Our Faith* (2003), and *An Intellectual in Public* (2003). Both *One Nation, After All* (1998) and *Moral Freedom* (2001) were selected as *New York Times* Notable Books of the Year.

INDEX

Culture: nature and meaning of, 18–22, 98–99; of politics, 90–93, 94

"Culture declinists," 75

Culture War? The Myth of a Polarized America (Fiorina), 6

Culture war hypothesis, 2–4, 12–16

Culture Wars: The Struggle to Define America (Hunter), 2, 3, 22, 104

Culture Wars for Contemporary Society (Brint), 27

Davis, Joseph, 93

Davis, Nancy, 17, 20, 84

Dean, Howard, 58, 70

Death of Character: Moral Education in an Age without Good and Evil (Hunter), 101

Declaration of Independence, 91

DeLay, Tom, 42, 49, 55

Democratic Party: and African Americans, 59–60; and Black churches, 52; and Catholics, 52; and economic issues, 58; and election of 2004, 32, 44–45, 52, 70; FDR coalition of, 50; and gay marriage, 58; and income gap, 88; and Iraq war, 70; and liberal activists, 57–58; and media, 51; and Modernist Mainline Protestants, 32; positions of, 53; and religio-cultural preferences, 32; and Schiavo case, 58

Deviancy, 78

Difference and liberalism, 10–13, 34–36

DiMaggio, Paul, 17, 20, 84

Dionne, E. J., Jr., 1–9, 46, 93, 95

Disparate social, moral, and political issues, 12

Dissensus: social composition of, 24–27; theoretical reflections on, 33–34

Divorce, 58, 77, 101

Dobson, James, 103

Douglas, Mary, 99

Dowd, Matthew, 84

Drinan, Robert, 52

Durkheim, Emile, 16, 21, 99

Dworkin, Ronald, 53, 57

Economic issues, 88

Edsall, Thomas Byrne, 3

Education, 13, 29, 30, 32, 81

Election of *1960*, 11, 60

Election of *1964*, 55

Election of *2000*, 50, 51, 63, 67–69

Election of *2004*: and abortion, 45–47, 103; assessment of, 43–48, 51, 54, 69–70, 93; and Catholics, 103–04; and culture war, 67, 74; and Democratic Party, 32, 44–45, 52, 54, 70; and gay marriage, 43–48, 92–93; and House of Representatives, 51; and income gap, 88; and moral values, 43–45, 54, 63, 68; and Nader, 50; and religio-cultural factors, 32; and Republican Party, 32, 44–45, 54, 58, 69–70, 92–93; and Schiavo case, 43; voter turnout in, 85

Election of *2006* (midterm), 48

Electoral college, 43, 51

Elites: cultural war fueled by, 7, 84–88, 97–98; influence on Middle America, 30–33; polarization of, 84–86; of progressive left, 24; self-importance of, 86; work of and institutions under, 27–28, 30, 31, 87

Enduring cultural war, 10–40

Entertainment. *See* Popular entertainment

Episcopal Church, 59, 102

Evangelical Christians: and election of *2004*, 70; and interfaith alliance, 3,

Individual virtue, 101
Institute for Advanced Studies in
  Culture, 23
Institutions of culture, 99
Intellectuals, 5, 74
Intelligent design, 30
Interfaith alliance, 3, 12, 16, 102–03,
  104
Internet, 75, 79–80
Iraq war, 43, 44, 45, 70
Ireland, independence of, 31
Islam, 66
Israel, 31, 104
"It's Morning After in America"
  (Hymowitz), 75

Jeffords, Jim, 50
Jews: and interfaith alliance, 3, 12, 16,
  102–03, 104; and liberal democracy,
  11; and Middle East conflict, 31;
  religious and political views of, 3, 52,
  60, 62, 102; and Republican Party,
  102
John Birch Society, 105
Journalism, 94
Judicial activists, 48, 57, 100
Judicial review, 53
"Justice Sunday," 53

Kennedy, John F., 11, 60
Kerry, John, 54, 103
Kulturkampf, 67
Kyoto Accord, 91

Land, Richard, 103
Language, 28
Liberal democracy, 11, 12, 95
Liberalism: and beginning of culture
  war, 53; cultural shift toward, 87, 95;
  and culture war, 53, 70; and

Democratic Party, 57–58; and
  difference, 10–13, 34–36; and
  divisions with conservatives, 74; and
  elites, 87; future of, 105, 106–07;
  and judicial review, 53; and media,
  51–52; positions of, 4–5, 10–11, 53;
  as traditionalists, 101–02
Lieberman, Joseph, 58, 98
Lobbying groups, 94
Locke, John, 106
Lott, Trent, 45
Lugar, Richard G., 1
Luhmann, Niklas, 99

Machen, J. Gresham, 61, 62
Magna Carta, 91
Majority party's role, 50
Maoist Revolution, 31
Market economy, 88
Marsden, George, 61
Marshall, Thurgood, 65
Marx, Karl, 16
Massachusetts Supreme Court on
  legalization of gay marriage, 47, 70
McCain, John, 70
McCarthy, Joseph, 105
Media, 51–52, 68
Medical marijuana, 85
Medicare, 85
Megachurches, 61, 103
Memoirs, 80
Middle East Conflict, 31
Middle portion of Americans, 4–5,
  31–32, 74, 87, 100–01. *See also*
  Ordinary Americans; Wolfe, Alan
Miller, Matthew, 85
Minority party's role, 50
Moore, Michael, 68
Morality: America's views on, 46;
  conception of what is, 23–24;

Reality TV shows, 79
Reed, Ralph, 57
Reiff, Philip, 104
Religion: and alliance among faiths, 3, 12, 16, 102–03; and culture war, 16, 52–53, 59–63; and education, 29, 30, 32, 81; and politics, 7, 49–58, 87, 102–03; and public life, 65–67; revival of, 60–61, 64; and Supreme Court, 65; traditionalists in, 102. *See also specific denominations and groups*
Republican National Convention (*1992*), 1
Republican Party: and African Americans, 59; and Catholics, 32, 52, 60, 102, 103–04; and Christian right, 70; and congressional districts, 50; conservatism of, 55; and conservative religious groups, 52–53, 102; and cultural politics, 92–93; and divorce, 58, 101; and election of *2004*, 32, 44–45, 58, 69–70, 92–93; and evangelical Christians, 32; and gay marriage, 47–48, 54; and impeachment of Clinton, 67, 86; and income gap, 88; and Jews, 102; and judicial activists, 57; and judicial appointments, 67; and media, 51; need for cultural war by, 54; objectives of, 53–54; and political contributions, 57, 98; and Protestants, 32, 52, 102, 103; and religio-cultural preferences, 32; and Schiavo case, 41–42, 43, 67, 70–71, 93; and Southern Baptist Convention, 52; Southern strategy of, 45, 50; and terrorist attacks, 69
Residence as sociological factor, 13
Rieff, Philip, 34
Right to die. *See* Schiavo, Terri

Robertson, Pat, 64
Robinson, Robert, 17, 20, 84
Roe v. *Wade* (*1973*), 46–47
Roosevelt, Franklin Delano, 50
Rove, Karl, 2, 51, 69, 70
Russian Revolution, 31
Rwanda, 31

Schiavo, Terri, 43–49; and conservatives, 56; and culture war, 30; and Democratic Party, 58; divisions caused by, 74; and elites, 7, 84, 85, 98; and ordinary Americans, 78, 84, 85, 93, 98; public opinion on, 41–42, 55; and Republican Party, 41–42, 43, 67, 70–71, 93
Schlesinger, Arthur, Jr., 93
Schools. *See* Education
Schwarzenegger, Arnold, 103
Secularism, 63–67
Self-help and religious faith, 63
September *11*th terrorist attacks, 69, 71, 75, 105
Sharon, Ariel, 104
Shields, Todd G., 44–46
Simmel, Georg, 16
Smith, Christian, 17, 20, 27, 84
"Social imaginaries," 91
Social order, 12–13
Social sciences and culture, 19–20, 86–87, 105
Social Security, 54, 85
Southern Baptist Convention, 52
Southern strategy of Republican Party, 45, 50
South Park (cable TV show), 76, 78
"South Park Conservatives," 76
Stem cell research, 7, 49, 55, 69, 70, 84, 85, 100
Sullivan, Andrew, 75